Landmark
BOOKS

D1255090

The Swamp Fox
of the Revolution

THE
SWAMP
FOX
OF THE REVOLUTION

by Stewart H. Holbrook

ILLUSTRATED BY ERNEST RICHARDSON

Random House • New York

Second Printing
© Copyright, 1959, by Stewart H. Holbrook
All rights reserved under International and Pan-American Copyright
Conventions. Published in New York by Random House, Inc., and
simultaneously in Toronto, Canada, by Random House of Canada, Limited.
Library of Congress Catalog Card Number: 59-12369
Manufactured in the United States of America
by H. Wolff, New York

For My Daughters
Sibyl Morningstar Holbrook
Bonnie Stewart Holbrook

CONTENTS

TO THE READER

There are few if any figures in American military history stranger than Francis Marion, and certainly none more appealing. A small wizened man who walked with a swaying limp, he was swarthy, eagle-nosed, careless of appearance, and no more communicative than an Indian.

In a day when cocked hats were the proper garb of American officers, General Marion fought through the Revolution wearing a battered little old helmet of the militia. In a day when rum was the drink of soldiers, Marion's canteen never held anything else than vinegar mixed with water.

With little help he organized a crowd of backwoodsmen into a brigade which without pay, often without enough ammunition and, living as they could off the country, carried on a practically private war against redcoats and Tories.

Marion's raids on their outposts and supply trains so troubled the British, who could never catch him, that they called him The Swamp Fox. Lurking in the dark marshlands until chance offered a target, he led his bushwhackers without warning out of the swirling mists to hit the enemy quickly and savagely, then disappeared into the trackless swamps.

When General Nathanael Greene came to head the southern department of the American army, South Carolina was in the tight fist of the British. Greene was quick to enlist the aid of Marion's little band of irregulars. They struck the enemy again and again, to such effect that Greene counted them of incomparable help in knocking out the chain of enemy forts, one after the other, until the British were driven to their last stand in Charleston, and from there sailed away to England.

Little wonder that in his native South Carolina, whose people have long memories and are happily given to remembrance of the heroes of the past, Francis Marion stands superb and unique—The Swamp Fox of the Revolution. He now belongs to the nation.

Stewart Holbrook

The Swamp Fox
of the Revolution

· I ·

THE SWAMP FOX GETS HIS NAME

The troop of Colonel Tarleton's British cavalry rode head-on into the dismal place and came to a confused halt as the legs of their horses sank knee-deep into the muck. This astonishing softness was the virtually bottomless bog that surrounded and protected the headquarters of General Francis Marion, commander of a bushwhacking brigade of American militia composed of South Carolinians.

The dashing Tarleton and his horsemen had been chasing Marion himself all the way from the upper reaches of the Black Mingo, and here they were now, in mid 1780, threshing helplessly in the savage jungle somewhere near the forks of the Pee Dee River and Lynchs Creek. And worse, their American quarry had suddenly disappeared into the mists that rose and swirled from the sluggish waters which stank from rotting vegetation.

The British troopers didn't know it, but even as their poor animals struggled in the mud and water,

Marion caught glimpses of the British splashing

Marion, unseen, was watching them from a bank of Snow Island just across the deep sullen stream.

They did not suspect there was anything like a solid island in this swamp world, yet there on dry ground stood Marion and his horse, hidden by mist, thicket and the immense beards of Spanish moss hanging from trees, peering at the distressed British. He caught glimpses of the men, in their handsome uniforms faced with red, splashing about in the deep

about in the deep gloom of the forest cover.

gloom of the forest cover. He felt certain they would not tarry long.

As the frightened horses reared and sank, the live oaks seemed to slap viciously at the riders, cutting their faces, knocking weapons from their hands. The unusual hubbub also stirred up sluggish reptilian life. Tarleton's men were startled to see snakes as thick as their upper arms drop from low-hanging limbs into the pools of scum, then go slithering away.

"God bless us," cried a young redcoat. "Even the serpents here take to the water!"

Just then, as a couple of the soldiers started to dismount, intending to stand on what looked to be a piece of the trunk of a fallen tree, the long greenish-brown object suddenly heaved and slid noiselessly into a deep pool, then disappeared beneath a line of hissing bubbles. The hair of the two men rose straight on end. They had just seen their first alligator.

Even Colonel Tarleton had had enough. "Come on, boys," he shouted. "Let's get out of here. The devil himself could not catch this swamp fox."

That was the way in which British Colonel Banastre Tarleton, commander of Lord Cornwallis' cavalry, came to speak the nickname that was to follow Francis Marion through the war and into history.

Francis Marion, The Swamp Fox. It was a nickname well earned. No American leader had more need to play fox than General Marion. Denied the fighting strength of a full regiment simply because there were not enough patriots to go around, he had instead to use the speed and cunning of the fox against superior forces.

When the watching Marion had seen Tarleton and his troopers get clear of the terrible mire and turn back to get out from the place, he mounted his horse and rode on toward his own camp in the middle of Snow Island. He soon met and saluted a picket who challenged him. Although a few such guards were posted around the hide-out, this was more for the sake of military discipline than because of danger from the enemy. Marion, who knew his home country much as Ethan Allen knew the Green Mountains, had chosen this island for his base of operations because he knew it could not be attacked by less than an army.

Snow Island was surrounded by the waters of

Lynchs Creek and the Pee Dee River. These streams were in turn surrounded by bayous and swamps and woods. They were impenetrable to all except natives like the hunters, trappers and backwoods farmers who made up the brigade organized by their old friend and neighbor, Francis Marion, recently given a South Carolina commission as brigadier general.

Here on the island there was fine grazing for horses. Here, too, General Marion had begun to accumulate modest stores of provisions such as corn and sweet potatoes, pork and beef, and salt. The latter had become so scarce in wartime it was worth almost its weight in gold. Another rarity was gunpowder. When Marion managed to get a small keg of it, the stuff was rationed to his men almost by the grain.

For several weeks past the island had been Marion's chief hide-out, commissary, and hospital. From here he had raided and otherwise harassed the British, even though the enemy had already defeated American General Benjamin Lincoln at Charleston, forcing his surrender and taking most of his Continental troops prisoner. In fact, Marion's men had so troubled the British Commander in Chief, Lord Cornwallis, that he had given orders to his cavalry chieftain, Tarleton, to run Marion and his hard-riding bushwhackers to earth and destroy them.

General Marion had recently run afoul of Tarleton by accident while returning from a scouting trip to the region between the Black Mingo and the Santee rivers, and the chase was on. It had been a fairly close call, but once again Marion had seemed to the British to disappear into thin air, or rather into the swamp mists.

Now safely in camp, Marion was greeted by one of his most trusted lieutenants, Colonel Peter Horry.

It was near supper time. Supper time for Marion's brigade was a Spartan meal. Like his men, General Marion sat down on a log to eat a piece of boiled beef and a roasted sweet potato served on a plate of oak bark. Instead of the tea his men liked, however, Marion sipped away at his canteen which held water mixed with vinegar. This was invariably the General's drink, in camp or on the field. How he came by this habit is anyone's guess, but it was an excellent practice. Back in the days of Julius Caesar, the Roman legions were issued vinegar as a part of their standard ration. It was a preventative against a skin disease, scurvy.

When the simple meal was over, Colonel Horry and the other field officers drew aside to hear what news their commander had brought. They grouped around Marion as he sat on a low stump, a stick in one of his hands tracing rough maps in the sand indicating where the various British troops were stationed and what they were doing.

There he sat in the gathering twilight, a small, almost frail figure, wizened, swarthy, eagle-nosed, with eyes as black as coals, wearing on his head a little round leather helmet bearing the silver crescent of the 2nd Carolina Infantry. Though that regiment was no longer in existence, Marion had a liking for the cap. It had served him well during early battles of the war, and he wore it still, even though it was badly charred on one side. But the crescent badge shone bright. On it you could read the bold legend, *Liberty or Death.*

The battered little cap was as much a part of Marion's uniform as the little sword which, though no man ever saw him draw it and it may well have rusted fast in the scabbard, still dangled from his belt.

The officers watched closely as General Marion traced the positions of the British camps with his stick. Being a man of very few words, he went to the heart of the matter. "Things are heading up for a big fight," he said. "Cornwallis is moving his army north to stop our new commander, General Gates. Congress sent him to take the place of General Lincoln."

Colonel Horry had a question. "Have you any idea where the big fight will be?" he asked.

"Somewhere northwest of here."

"Up on the Wateree?" Horry suggested the name of the river.

"Possibly," replied Marion. "The way I heard it, Cornwallis expects to meet Gates around Camden."

Marion drew a few more lines with his stick. "The British supply line to Camden," he explained, "runs north along the Santee. Our brigade is going to cut that line."

General Marion had it right. There *was* going to be a big fight. After the American disaster at Charleston, and the destruction or capture of Lincoln's entire army, Congress had directed Horatio Gates, hero of the great victory over the British at Saratoga, to take command of the American forces in the Southern Department of the Army.

It was greatly to Gates's credit that he accepted the

With a stick, Marion traced rough maps in the sand.

assignment without protest. It was a tough one. The only patriot forces left in South Carolina were a few scattered irregulars like the men with Marion, others with Colonel Thomas Sumter, and a few more who, taken all together, probably did not equal the number of Carolina Tories, as the residents who favored the British were known. In short, what Congress grandly called "the Southern Department of the Army" was pretty much a myth.

But General Gates did not arrive alone in South Carolina. He came at the head of more than 3,000 soldiers, among them veterans from Maryland and Delaware, a large number of untried Virginia militia, and a regiment of North Carolinians.

That had been a long month ago, and Marion and Peter Horry had ridden to meet the famous new commander and offer their services.

But Gates had waved them away, possibly because they did not look like Gates's idea of officers. "Sir," he told his adjutant, "say to them we already have enough men for our purposes." It is doubtful if any general was ever more mistaken than Gates.

But despite the fact that the new commander of the Southern Department had refused Marion's proffer of aid, that officer did not sulk. He would do his best to prevent ammunition and other supplies from reaching Cornwallis before the big fight came off.

And now, sitting with his men in the Snow Island hide-away, General Marion gave orders to break camp next day. He was prepared to ride overland to the Santee River.

"We'll head for Nelson's Ferry," he told his officers. "That's a likely place to catch redcoats crossing the river." He was silent a few moments. "If Gates won't let us fight at Camden," he said, "we shall try to cut the British line of supply. Soldiers can't fight well without something to eat—or without powder."

That was a long speech for a man as sparing of words as Francis Marion, beside whom an Indian was talkative.

The simple council of war was over. Colonel Horry passed the word to the men. "Breakfast before daylight," he said. "All hands in the saddle, ready to ride, at sunup."

Dark fell over the camp on Snow Island in the great swamp. By midnight the campfires had burned down to a few glowing coals that looked to the lonely pickets like small red eyes blinking at them in the darkness.

· II ·

MARION'S BRIGADE
IN ACTION

While his men were sleeping soundly this night, their chieftain lay wakeful on his bed of boughs and grass. As the dark hours moved slowly ahead, General Marion was silently reviewing events that left him somewhat anxious about the outcome of the "big fight" brewing between Gates and Cornwallis.

The American situation in South Carolina had been growing steadily worse almost since the Revolution began in 1775. In that year Marion had left his small plantation, Pond Bluff, to serve in the provincial con-

15

gress which drew up a state constitution and elected John Rutledge governor and Henry Laurens lieutenant governor.

The courageous members of this meeting also voted to raise three regiments of militia. Marion, a veteran of the campaign against the Cherokees during the French and Indian War of earlier years, was elected a captain in the 2nd Regiment whose colonel was William Moultrie. Another captain was Peter Horry, friend and neighbor of Marion.

Returning to their home district on the Santee River, Marion and Horry started at once to muster their neighbors into the 2nd Regiment. Many of the recruits were, like Marion and Horry, descendants of French Protestants called Huguenots who had been forced to flee France late in the seventeenth century. All of them were familiar with firearms, for in those days men shot the animals that provided the meat for their table. But Captains Marion and Horry had to make *soldiers* of the men. This took a lot of doing.

The 2nd Regiment fought bravely during Moultrie's brilliant defense of Charleston against the British fleet which had been sent to capture the capital of South

Carolina. Operating from forts made of palmetto logs and hastily erected on islands in the harbor, the patriots crippled the whole fleet, which soon gave up and sailed away.

But not far. The British had no idea of giving up the South. They returned promptly and captured the important Georgia port of Savannah. Then they lay siege to Charleston.

Defending the city was the army of General Benjamin Lincoln. His soldiers held it until their ammunition gave out, food gave out, and finally even drinking water had to be rationed. Lincoln surrendered. Some of his men became prisoners of war. Others were permitted to return to their homes after swearing they would no longer bear arms against their King, George III.

Captain Marion escaped capture because, just before the surrender, he suffered a broken ankle and had, with other officers unfit for duty, been ordered to leave the city. He made his way to the swamp country near his plantation at Pond Bluff, where he hid out while his injury healed.

Meanwhile, Lord Cornwallis with 4,000 troops, including cavalry under Colonel Tarleton, went to work to stamp out any patriots who might still be found in South Carolina.

To oppose Cornwallis, the Continental Congress at Philadelphia now sent to South Carolina General Horatio Gates. He was so sure of himself, as we have seen, that he could not find a place in his army for either Peter Horry or the frail, wizened little man, Francis Marion.

But if Gates knew nothing of Marion's ability, such was not the case with Governor John Rutledge of South Carolina. He asked Marion to take command of a brigade to be raised among patriot farmers and to do what he could to harass the British.

New Brigadier General Marion and his friends worked swiftly. Within little more than a week, British Major Gainey, leading a regiment of Tory troops, was set upon at Britton's Neck on the Pee Dee River in a surprise attack. His men were well shot up and routed in the first engagement staged by Marion's still small command.

Marion's brigade did not lose a man. And the South

Carolinians captured a supply of powder sufficient to fill their nearly empty flasks and horns.

When word of the attack on Gainey reached Cornwallis, he was astonished that any "rebels" at all were left in the region. He ordered his cavalry commander, Tarleton, to take steps to discourage them.

Within twenty-four hours Marion struck again, this time attacking a larger force of Tories under Captain Barefield. Because the enemy outnumbered his men more than two to one, Marion did not want to fight on equal terms. Sending a small party ahead to attack, then to pretend to retreat, he prepared an ambush that caught the Tories off guard. Several were killed, more wounded, and the survivors were sent fleeing in every direction.

Again Cornwallis demanded that these bushwhacking rebels be stopped. Although both actions had been small, they forced the British commander in chief to realize that he was not operating in a completely conquered province.

For the first time since Charleston fell, the patriots really were stirring, even though to frighten them

Tarleton had begun to raid and burn their homes, to run off their horses and cattle, and to shoot all who attempted to defend their property. Threaten as he would, however, Tarleton was unable to find a single Tory who said he could guide the British through the swamps to the hide-out of General Marion.

Now, in that hide-out on Snow Island, sleepless General Marion watched while his brigade roused for breakfast in the early light of dawn. Small birds were sounding their first calls of the day. From somewhere deep in the swamp came the booming salute of a bittern. But no bugles were blown, no drums were sounded. More than a hundred of Marion's men quietly fed their horses, then squatted around to eat their sidemeat and corn bread.

The first blaze of the sun was just fighting through the mist as they mounted and rode slowly over the complicated route out of the terrible swamp that protected Snow Island. Long before noon they had reached the Black Mingo, forded it, and moved on to the Black River.

Here the column stopped briefly. Marion and Peter

With a small party, Marion prepared an ambush.

Horry conferred; then Horry and a small detachment left the main body and struck out southwest. They were to destroy all boats and canoes found along the Lower Santee River. If possible, they were to buy or beg some much needed gunpowder and buckshot and send them to Marion. He and the brigade continued on toward the Upper Santee, his object the busy crossing called Nelson's Ferry.

Before Marion's column reached the Santee, it was overtaken by a hard-riding courier—sent possibly by the alert Governor Rutledge—with news of a disaster: The "big fight" had already come off. The armies of Gates and Cornwallis had met at Camden. The Americans had suffered a terrible and total defeat.

The dispatch informed Marion that Gates and those of his men who had not been killed, seriously wounded or captured were in flight to North Carolina. General Gates himself had ridden seventy desperate miles to escape. Nor was that all. Tarleton's troopers had paid especial attention to Colonel Thomas Sumter's company of patriots, taking more than half of them prisoner and killing many of the rest.

It was an American disaster of a size to discourage almost anyone. It meant that Marion was the only patriot commander still at large in South Carolina. The news must have made him feel terribly alone. If so, he gave no sign of it.

But his men must not know the truth. Not yet, anyway. The little general remained outwardly impassive, though his beady black eyes may have taken on added light. He told Colonel Hugh Horry, Peter's brother, to ride with him at the head of the column.

The column moved ahead toward the Upper Santee. Night found Marion's men approaching Nelson's Ferry. A halt was ordered, and scouts were sent forward to see what was happening along the river. The scouts were soon back, reporting that less than a mile distant there was a large convoy of American prisoners who had been taken at the battle of Camden. They were on their way to the British prison ships standing off Charleston. General Marion questioned a scout-sergeant.

"Yes, sir," replied the sergeant, "they seem to have camped for the night."

"What about pickets and guards?"

"Both are posted."

"Lots of pickets?" General Marion asked.

"I can't be sure, sir. I know that the British officers have taken quarters in a house near the ferry. It looked as if they had stacked their arms just outside the door. But guards are walking post around the house. I think pickets have been set out, too."

General Marion dismissed the sergeant-scout. He had decided at once what to do: He would attack the encampment just at dawn and free the American prisoners. He ordered Colonel Hugh Horry and sixteen men to circle the British position, then to approach the house from the far side. He himself and the rest of the brigade would come up from the near side.

The moon had waned into a pale sky as Horry and his detail took off through the swamp. When Marion figured sufficient time had elapsed, he led the main body forward. They were still some distance from the house when they heard a shot followed by shouts and the pounding hoofs of horses.

What had happened was that an alert British picket had caught sight of Horry's party and given warning. There was nothing Horry could do but to attack, whether or not Marion and the main troop were near enough to give support.

"Come on, boys!" Horry shouted. "Charge 'em!" Yelling like Indians, the sixteen horsemen charged.

The camp was thrown into confusion. Many there must have thought Horry was leading a small army. Before Marion could come up, Horry's crew shot down the guards at the house. Jumping to the ground, Horry placed six of his men to guard the stacked weapons, and then led the other ten into the house where the British officers were barely waking. They surrendered.

Before the British pickets and other soldiers outside knew what was happening, they were attacked from the front by Marion's men, who came in shooting. It was all over quickly. The redcoats threw down their arms. The half-starved American prisoners milled about, weeping with joy at their rescue from the fate of being held in the dreaded prison hulks the British had waiting for them in Charleston harbor.

It was a brilliant raid. One hundred and fifty Continental soldiers, all Marylanders, were freed from the victors of Camden.

Though grateful to their rescuers, the former prisoners of course told Marion's men of the American disaster, news of which Marion had carefully kept from them. But now, Marion's soldiers were also told by the Marylanders of the poor American generalship displayed in the battle with Cornwallis.

Marion had, naturally enough, hoped that many if not all of the Marylanders would join his brigade. He was sadly disappointed. Most of the Maryland Continentals had had enough of war. They were going home as best they could. They said that the war in the South was already lost. Only three of them accepted Marion's invitation to join his force.

Only three out of one hundred and fifty—it was disheartening. Worse, the defeatist talk of the released Marylanders depressed many of Marion's men. On the march back to the Pee Dee, more than a dozen asked the General's permission to go home. They were very

Horry led his men into the house where the British

worried about their families, now that British control of South Carolina seemed complete—or complete except for this very brigade that they were leaving. Marion let them go.

"I want no men who are soldiers against their will," he told his brigade.

When the brigade got back to Snow Island, with depleted ranks, their General knew that every man who remained would be with him until the end.

But what Marion now faced was the fact that his

officers were barely waking. They surrendered.

so-called brigade had shrunk to less than seventy men. And no matter how good they were, what could seventy men do against a powerful opposing force? The 63rd Regiment of British Regulars, with an added force of Tories, had now been sent into the Williamsburg district between the Pee Dee and the Santee rivers with orders to wipe out the last patriot resistance.

In command of this force, as General Marion was soon informed, was Major James Wemyss, an able officer and possibly as ruthless a man as the British Army contained. With more than one thousand men, he began at once to make his weight felt.

With information supplied by Tory spies, Wemyss singled out the homes and farms of suspected patriots for immediate attention. One by one he ordered the victims to vacate their houses. Then he permitted his soldiers to enter and take whatever they wanted. And then orders were given to set the houses and barns on fire.

Sweeping through the Kingstree community on Black River, Wemyss's soldiers left a trail of smoking ruins. Knowing it was worse than useless to attack with seventy men, Marion sent Major John James to scout the district. James returned and reported that his own home had just been burned on Wemyss's orders. Everything on the plantation had been despoiled, and even James's modest library of books had been piled on the flames.

Within another month Wemyss, apparently in the belief that he had taught the Williamsburg patriots a lesson, marched his main command to Georgetown on the coast. He left Captain John Ball with a force of several hundred Tories stationed at Shepard's Ferry on Black Mingo River, with orders to police the region.

Although Captain Ball knew that Francis Marion was hiding out somewhere, he was unworried. The patriot cause in South Carolina was in so weak a condition that it seemed unlikely any rebel would dare to raise his hand.

Wemyss had shot and hacked and burned fear of King George III into the hearts of the inhabitants. Lord Cornwallis had defeated their Commander in Chief, Gates. Charleston and Georgetown were in British hands.

Neither Cornwallis nor Wemyss nor Ball ever heard

of Snow Island. There the last patriot leader left in the province—or state—had retired with his entire command which numbered less than seventy men.

If so much as an ember of hope survived anywhere in South Carolina, it would have to be fanned, if at all, by the Swamp Fox of Snow Island.

· III ·

VICTORY AT TARCOTE
SWAMP

Lying idle for four weeks on Snow Island gave both
men and horses some much needed rest. After that,
however, they grew restless. Some of the men, bored
by inaction, asked permission to "go home for a few
days." Within a short time a muster of the brigade
showed that its strength had fallen to no more than
fifty men and officers.

Several of the officers had begun to urge General
Marion to attack Captain John Ball and his Tories.
Though such spirit did Marion's heart good, he was

too level-headed a commander to fall in with the proposal. He knew that Ball's Tories numbered at least
nine hundred, perhaps a full thousand. To lead fifty
men against them would be the same as committing
his brigade to mass suicide.

"No," Marion told his impatient officers. "We've
got to wait a bit. Some of our boys will be back soon."

A few of them did return, but what electrified every-
body on Snow Island was a piece of fast and inspired
work by Major John James. Marion had sent James
out through the settlements to raise new recruits. And
now, unannounced, he returned to the hide-out leading almost one hundred mounted men. They had been
induced to join the brigade by the efforts of James's
cousin, Captain John James, and his friend Captain
Henry Mouzon.

Not all the new men had muskets. Many carried
fowling pieces. A few had no firearms at all, but rode
into camp with swords that had been pounded out at
home from scythes.

Although his somber face never changed expression,
Marion was nevertheless elated. Here, he thought,
were just the kind of men he wanted to free South

Carolina from British troops and their Tory allies.

While the newcomers were getting settled in camp, Major James took General Marion aside. "These boys," he said, "agreed to join chiefly because Captains James and Mouzon promised them they would be fighting Tories in no time at all."

"But they're pretty green," the General observed. "Have any of them ever been under fire?"

"Oh, yes. Quite a number of them have been in skirmishes with the Tories. A few were in the old 2nd Regiment at the defense of Charleston."

"That is all very well," replied Marion, "but we shall have to get guns for those boys who are toting swords."

Colonel Hugh Horry came up. "Our scouts report that all of Captain Ball's Tories have muskets," he said.

General Marion did a rare thing; he smiled. "You mean we ought to attack Ball and take those muskets away from him?" he asked.

"Well," said Horry, "it might work. I don't think Ball's well-armed crew have smelled powder yet."

General Marion was not at all sure it was wise to attack Ball, but he understood the temper of his own men. He knew they had grown so impatient there was danger that even more of them would ask permission to "go home for a few days." His command could not stand many more such furloughs.

The General called a council of war. Colonel Horry favored an attack on Ball at once. Captains James and Mouzon, who had scouted Ball's position, indicated how a surprise attack might be made.

Two nights later General Marion and one hundred and fifty men approached Shepard's Ferry on the Black Mingo. The ferry itself proved to be well guarded. Ball's camp was on the far side of the river, where the water was too deep to be forded. With Captain James guiding, the brigade moved a mile or so north toward the only bridge in the neighborhood.

Advance scouts came in to say the way was clear; there were no pickets at the bridge. Riding single-file, Marion led his men across the narrow structure of loose planks. Before he had gone ten yards he knew the attack could not be a surprise. The planks were fairly booming from the impact of hoofs. In the dark quiet of the night they echoed like thunder. Yet it was too late to do anything but go on.

Before quite half the brigade had cleared the bridge, Marion heard a musket shot somewhere downriver. This was what he had feared. An alert Tory picket had given warning.

Giving rein to his horse, who leaped ahead, Marion with Captain James at his side led the brigade at a gallop toward a farmhouse which they knew to be Captain Ball's headquarters.

They could see the building looming up in the dark. But there were no lights either in or around the house. Marion brought his men to a halt. "They are ready and waiting for us," he said to Captain James.

Quickly and quietly Marion gave orders. All except a small troop of officers who were not attached to specific companies dismounted. The mounted officers were sent up the road to make a frontal attack on the house. Two companies under Colonel Hugh Horry and Captain John James moved to the right and the left to support the main attack from the flanks. Marion and a fourth party waited where they stood.

Before the mounted officers had reached the house, which they found deserted, Horry's company ran headlong into the main body of Tories well hidden on the edge of a field. And before the startled Americans could get their guns to their shoulders, the Tories poured a frightful volley into their ranks.

"Down, down!" Horry shouted. "Shoot from the ground!" By then the Tories let go another volley, and Horry's men began tumbling. But some of Horry's men were shooting, too.

Captain John James's company, which had met no sign of the enemy on their side of the house, came running to support their comrades, some of whom were giving way.

"Stand fast!" James cried. Then the field lit up with the fire James's men turned on the enemy. And Horry's hard-pressed soldiers did stand fast.

So did the Tories, as their commander John Ball rallied them in the face of this new danger from the flank. They stood up well, too, and were holding their own when General Marion and the reserves came in yelling and shooting.

Captain Ball fell, mortally wounded. His men hesitated, unsure what to do. Marion's men began swinging their wicked sabers. It was just too much for the enemy's green troops. The Tories turned almost as one man, scattering into the swampy woods that bordered the battlefield.

It was all over, and for so brief a fight it had been a deadly affair. Sixty Tories lay dead on the ground near where their brave Captain Ball had fallen.

The Tories poured a frightful volley into their ranks.

The brigade had won the fight—at terrible cost. More than fifty of Marion's men were killed or badly wounded. Among them was Captain George Logan who, on the day before, had risen from his sickbed and ridden eighty miles in order to be with his old friend, General Marion, in this bloody affair at Shepard's Ferry. Captain Henry Mouzon was so badly wounded he was unfit for further service in the war.

Out of this battle, too, came a horse soon to become famous. He had belonged to gallant Captain John Ball, the Tory commander. A big sorrel as intelligent as he was good to look at, he was presented to General Marion, who named him "Ball" on the spot and rode him throughout the rest of the struggle.

It is worth knowing that the horse named Ball was, like his new owner, a natural leader. When, as often happened, it was necessary for the brigade to swim a river, many inexperienced horses feared to enter deep water, and balked. General Marion astride Ball would then take the lead, and the sorrel seemed to "float over the stream like an amphibious animal," as Major John James remembered it. The rest of the horses soon learned to follow Ball instinctively.

Smoke from this small and costly battle at Shepard's Ferry had little more than cleared when a patriot spy came looking for General Marion to report that a notorious Tory named Colonel Tynes was recruiting farmers in the Black River region.

"Where is Tynes's headquarters?" Marion asked the spy.

"Well, he is sort of camping at Tarcote, near the fork of Black River."

"How many men has he with him?"

"I don't know," the spy answered. "I didn't see more than a hundred or so. But more were coming in every little while."

"What about muskets? Are his men all armed?" Marion asked.

"Yes, sir, they sure got guns. Lots of guns. I see some powder kegs, too. A feller I talked with told me Colonel Tynes has got everything."

"What do you mean, everything?" asked Marion.

"The feller said they even got saddles and bridles for all hands. He says they got plenty ammunition. Lots of grub, too."

It all sounded to General Marion just a little too good. Yet even if it were only half true, the brigade certainly could use some of those saddles and bridles and muskets and food. He was tempted. A fast raid might capture enough equipment and arms to put his men on a par with their enemies. What was more, Marion felt the time had come to make a supreme effort to discourage Tory sentiment. The patriot cause in South Carolina was weak enough.

General Marion called his officers together. As soon as dark fell the brigade would ride to Tarcote at the fork of Black River. Hugh Horry and a small troop would scout ahead. The plan was to hit the Tory camp a little after midnight. It must be a surprise attack.

With Horry and his scouts a couple of miles in advance, Marion's battered but cheerful command moved through the night. Close to eleven o'clock Marion halted his men. All dismounted to await word from Hugh Horry. It was nearly midnight when the scouts came in. The report was almost unbelievably good.

"I never saw the like of it before," Colonel Horry told Marion. "Maybe they've got plenty of arms and ammunition, but they just aren't soldiers yet."

"No pickets?" asked Marion.

"Not a picket, not a guard of any kind. We got close enough to their campfires to learn as much. We could see those Tories, many of them rolled up in

blankets, asleep. Others were drinking rum and play-
ing cards around the fires."

"See anything of Colonel Tynes?"

"Nary a hair. I reckon he was taking a nap."

General Marion gave the order. The brigade moved
ahead, the horses walking, until enemy campfires
could be seen through the trees. Men and officers dismounted, tethered the animals, then spread out in a
half circle. Horry shot his pistol into the air. At the
signal Marion's men rushed in, yelling like Cherokees
and shooting.

The surprise was complete. Scarcely half a dozen
Tories had a chance to fire before the patriots closed in
with swords and bayonets. No patriot was hit. Only
two Tories were killed, and eight wounded.

Marion's brigade did not have time to reload before Colonel Tynes and many of his men threw
down their weapons and raised their arms in surrender. The others disappeared into the Tarcote
swamp.

Here was a victory to cheer Marion as nothing before had done. It couldn't be called a battle. It was a
raid. Yet from one viewpoint it was the most impor-

tant engagement the brigade had won. Taking stock of the Tory supplies that had so easily fallen into his hands, General Marion saw that at last his men were to be as well equipped as the troops of the Continental Army.

The victory cheered Marion as nothing before had done.

The men were delighted. They ate Tory food, they drank Tory liquids, while a quartermaster detail sorted the muskets, pistols, swords, and a few bridles and saddles. There was also a stock of powder, bullets, and flints. The booty included even a drum and a bugle.

Some of the men in the brigade were yelling, demanding to be allowed to go off into the swamp to run down the fleeing Tories. Marion gave orders that no man should leave camp. He knew well enough that the difference between many Tories and patriots was slim. All wanted to be on the stronger side, whichever side it was. King or Congress did not mean much to them. The way to make patriots, Marion believed, was to show that patriots were unbeatable and that the Tories, in the long run, were bound to lose.

"Let them run, let them hide," he told his soldiers. "One of these days, mark my words, they will be ready to turn patriot. They will be fighting on our side."

On the afternoon after the raid, General Marion had twenty-one prisoners brought before him and told them that any who would swear not to take up arms again against the American cause would be released on the spot.

All took the oath on the spot. Several asked to join

Marion's brigade then and there. They were accepted without further ado.

If it seems strange to us today that Marion was willing to have turncoats for soldiers, it was not strange in that time and place. It is a matter of record that many of Tynes's Tories who fled during the raid soon came to join Marion and fought bravely for the American cause thereafter.

Two days after the Tarcote raid, Marion's brigade, armed and equipped as never before, and accompanied by packhorses loaded with ammunition and other supplies, rode happily into the hide-out on Snow Island. It was now late October, 1780.

During the next week, two trusted patriot couriers made their way to Snow Island with dispatches for General Marion. The first message contained glorious news: A large force of backwoodsmen of what are now Tennessee and West Virginia, with other patriots of North Carolina, and led by Colonel Isaac Shelby, Lieut-Colonel Jack Sevier, Lieut-Colonel Benjamin Cleveland and others, had attacked eleven

hundred Tories and Britishers under Major Patrick
Ferguson at King's Mountain, North Carolina, and
won a spectacular victory.

Major Ferguson and several hundred Tories were
killed. The victory was marred by the hanging of
nine Tories who, rightly or wrongly, were suspected
of having committed similar outrages on patriots in
the past. But the victory was so great that Lord Cornwallis, who had started to move his main army north,
heading into Virginia, had to change his tactics. The
Carolinas were not, after all, completely under British control. Cornwallis turned in his tracks and retreated south, going into winter quarters at Winnsboro, South Carolina.

The second message for General Marion, which
came a few days later, reported that Colonel Banastre
Tarleton had been ordered to return to the Williamsburg district between the Pee Dee and the Santee
rivers and to stay there until he had wiped out General Marion and his so-called brigade.

The commander of the so-called brigade read of
this new threat with unusual interest. Taking a sip

of his vinegar ration, he remarked to Colonel Peter Horry that he was pleased Tarleton had waited until Marion's men had equipped themselves with the fine weapons and other supplies furnished by the Tories in the Tarcote raid.

· IV ·

ATTACK ON GEORGETOWN
FAILS

It was well that Marion and his men got what cheer they could from the new weapons and supplies they captured from the Tories at Tarcote. There was little enough cheer elsewhere among the Americans, north or south.

As the latter months of 1780 dropped swiftly away into the past, the nation entered its blackest period since the Revolution began. The whole country was staggered by news of the treason of General Benedict Arnold. This trusted American officer had agreed, for cash, to deliver into British hands the important fortress of West Point, guardian of the Hudson River. Not only that. He had promised also to arrange for the capture of General George Washington.

It was a plot to shock and put fear into the staunchest patriot. That it failed was due only to the chance capture of one of Arnold's secret agents together with complete evidence of the whole shameful affair.

In this great crisis General Washington, already bearing burdens beyond knowing, rose to full stature and acted with what history has proved to be magnificent judgment.

First of all, there was the terrible mess in South Carolina. General Horatio Gates must be relieved of the command in the South. And if for no other reason than that both Gates, and General Benjamin Lincoln before him, had failed miserably to stop Cornwallis, the officer to supplant Gates must be without fail the best man possible.

General Washington had no doubts as to the best man possible. He was Major General Nathanael Greene. It is well to know something of the new commander of the Southern Department, for from this point on Francis Marion was to play an increasingly important part in the war.

Called the "Rhode Island Ironmaster" because of his peacetime occupation, Greene was born a Quaker but was "dropped from the Society of Friends" because he took part in a military parade, which was against Quaker principles.

Having served in the colonial militia, Greene was made a brigadier general in 1775, and was with the Continental Army during the siege of Boston. After the British evacuation of that city he was put in command of the army of occupation.

Though he had limped from a stiff knee since childhood, he was vigorous and an outstanding combat officer. It was Greene who, on that famous Christmas Eve at Trenton in 1776, had led the column under Washington which surprised and captured the Hessian regiments. He went on to suffer with his troops during the terrible winter at Valley Forge. He was also in the thick of battle at Germantown and Monmouth.

This was the soldier whom Washington now asked to take command of the department which, up till then, had seen its first Continental officer and his army defeated and captured, and the army of its second Continental chieftain routed and scattered.

In Charlotte, North Carolina, where he arrived on December 2, 1780, Major General Nathanael Greene was observed by the remnants of Gates's army to be a big-shouldered man with a florid face, blue eyes, a Grecian nose, and gracious manners. He seemed to radiate confidence. He quickly found that although the remnants of Gates's army toted up, on paper, to about twenty-three hundred men, less than eight hundred were fit and equipped for duty.

Greene also discovered other discouraging things. In the camp were rations for only three days. All army wagons had vanished somewhere, probably at the disastrous battle of Camden; so had most of the American artillery.

The soldiers themselves looked even worse than Greene had anticipated. Their clothing was pretty much in tatters. Their shoes were downright deplorable. Morale was, quite naturally, about as low as morale could get.

There were, however, a certain few assets that Greene was quick to recognize. One was young Colonel William Washington, a third cousin of the American commander in chief and a most able combat officer. Another was the huge Daniel Morgan, dressed in buckskins and, although creaky with rheumatism, determined to lead troops into whatever fight was offered.

On the way south, and expected any day, was Colonel Harry (Light-Horse) Lee, with his well-known Legion of fighting horsemen newly equipped with green jackets, white breeches, and plumed leather helmets.

Still another asset, one that General Gates had failed to recognize, was the brigade of bushwhackers led by Francis Marion. On his second day in Charlotte, General Greene sent greetings to General Marion, saying. "I have not the honor of your acquaintance, but am no stranger to your character and merit."

General Greene also proposed that Marion plan and lead an attack on British-held Georgetown on the coast. Then, as if to show the faith he placed in

The transports were soon loaded, and the Snow Island

Marion, Greene dispatched Colonel Lee and his Legion of well-trained horse soldiers to help with the attack.

Lee had a hard time of it even to locate Marion. Riding down from the Cheraws district on the upper Pee Dee River, Lee and his Legion were lost a dozen times before they stumbled by luck onto one of the Swamp Fox's foraging parties and were guided to Snow Island.

This meeting of the dashing, handsome, genial Lee, and the silent Marion, who spoke only when necessary, appealed to the imagination of Bruce Lancaster, the noted historian of the Revolution. Lee's

navy cast off for the voyage to Georgetown.

eyes, he thought, "must have bulged" as the reserved little man, "eternally sipping his favorite vinegar," gave orders to set the wheels turning for the move on Georgetown.

Muttering cryptic words, Marion sent messengers slipping away like shadows from Snow Island. The fascinated Lee could only guess as to what the errands were. No bugles were blown, no drums beaten. Yet the spoken orders of this chieftain of the swamps were being transmitted by couriers moving through the mists heavy with rot and the musky reek of alligators.

Within less than twenty-four hours the results of

Marion's orders began to be seen. The river became alive. Out of hidden creeks, from plantation landings, from unseen backwaters came a procession of canoes and rafts and boats and scows, paddled or rowed or poled by old men, half-grown boys, and women. These craft formed the navy, brought suddenly into being, to carry the several hundred foot soldiers and supplies down the Pee Dee to Georgetown on tidewater, at Winyah Bay.

Colonel Lee, a man of the world, could only marvel at such magic in the swamps.

The transports were soon loaded with men, equipment and provisions, and the Snow Island navy cast off for the voyage downriver. Lee's horsemen, guided by Marion's mounted men, started riding down the banks.

The combined forces reached Georgetown quickly and, in the early hours of morning, met in the rice fields near the British position. But due to the error of a guide, the Americans landed squarely among the guardposts beyond the barracks. An alert sentry gave the alarm. The soldiers roused and ran for the stone forts so quickly that only a few were hit by American bullets.

Colonel Lee urged sending his well-tested men against the barricaded British. But Marion knew the danger of attacking men who could shoot through the portholes of bullet-proof forts. He rejected Lee's suggestion. "It would cost too many lives," he said.

With neither artillery nor scaling ladders, the Americans were helpless. They withdrew. The cavalry and the flotilla returned upstream to Snow Island.

Georgetown did not fall. Yet the attack was far from being a total failure. The British, fearful from the close call, decided not to send any of their garrison north to operate with Cornwallis against General Greene. Indeed, it turned out that the commandant at Georgetown demanded reinforcements which otherwise would have been sent to help Cornwallis.

The raid achieved more than that. It was of really great value in proving to the American commander that regular and irregular troops *could* work together. Marion's men noticed and appreciated the value of formal discipline displayed by Lee's soldiers. Lee's Legion was amazed to see how fast and silently a large body of troops could be moved when backwoods conditions were understood and respected. And Lee and Marion had taken an immediate liking to each other. The Georgetown raid laid the foundation for future operations that were to be most profitable.

· V ·

WHAT HAPPENED AT
THE COWPENS

While Marion and Lee were preparing and carrying out the attack on Georgetown, General Greene was looking hard at the overall conditions facing him as the new commander of the Southern Department of the Army. The conditions were not good.

Several of Greene's staff thought it best to go into winter quarters. This meant that no action could be taken until spring. They pointed out, in favor of this plan, that Cornwallis had just received important reinforcements under General Alexander Leslie. These were mostly high-quality troops, including a brigade of Guards, a regiment of Highlanders, and some Hessian infantry.

"Sir," said one of Greene's officers, "Cornwallis can now put no less than four thousand men into the field. Trained soldiers. Better by far that we should lay low and recruit and train more men before we take on the British."

"In two or three months," added another of the staff, "we could muster troops enough to have a chance against Cornwallis."

"What you say is doubtless true," General Greene replied, "yet I fear the inactivity of winter quarters even more than superior numbers of the enemy."

Grizzled old Dan Morgan spoke up. "I'd rather fight," he said, "than to hole up all winter."

General Greene agreed with Morgan. "I have seen too many troops rot through too many winters," he said. "I do not dare do otherwise than to begin some action immediately."

General Morgan nodded. "I'm rusty enough," he said, "without sitting around till spring."

General Greene now turned to the reports of his

scouts and spies. They indicated that Cornwallis had concentrated the major body of his forces in and near Winnsboro. He had sent detachments to strengthen the stout British fort called Ninety-Six, on the Saluda River, and the British post at Camden on the Wateree.

Knowing he was not strong enough to attack the British at Camden, to say nothing of Winnsboro and Ninety-Six, General Greene decided to take what he knew was a grave risk: He would split up his own meager troops. His less ready men would go into training in the Cheraws district of the upper Pee Dee. His fittest soldiers would be sent on a march, under General Dan Morgan, with the hope of decoying part of the British out of Winnsboro.

Should Cornwallis suspect the ruse and set forth to attack Greene and his weak force in the Cheraws, instead of going after Morgan, then all was lost. If, however, he moved against the decoy troops, Morgan would at least have a chance to hurt Cornwallis in a hit-and-run attack.

As Greene outlined the plans, Dan Morgan, who had been promoted to brigadier general only a short while before, indicated his pleasure. Though stiff joints prevented him from getting into the saddle without a helping hand, this veteran who had commanded his own sharpshooters against Burgoyne at Saratoga and wanted "one more chance at the redcoats" was still a dangerous man to face.

Now General Morgan got into his famous buckskin shirt, was hoisted onto his horse, and rode out of American headquarters at the head of six hundred men, heading northwest. To cover his advance, Greene detailed Colonel William Washington and a body of troopers.

Two days later, Colonel James McCall, with two hundred and fifty South Carolina militiamen, joined Morgan's forces, and was sent under Colonel Washington to strike at a troublesome Tory party operating along Fairfort Creek. They surprised the Tories, made short work of them, then moved south across the Tyger and Enoree rivers as if they planned to attack Ninety-Six on the Saluda. Then they quickly turned back to join Morgan.

Cornwallis was first puzzled, then alarmed. What was Morgan up to? Was he actually leading Greene's main army into this northwest sector of South Carolina where the British maintained three important posts?

The British commander in chief did not hesitate. He sent Tarleton's superbly trained and equipped Dragoons, together with several pieces of artillery—some twelve hundred men in all—to take care of Morgan. As for that seasoned old fighter, he selected a spot which he hoped would induce Tarleton to attack him.

This was a level stretch of timbered country where the trees stood so far apart that horsemen could easily ride among them—a parklike area almost, used in former days by drovers to rest and graze their cattle. It was known as the Cowpens.

On this Cowpens plain were two low hills. On the higher hill General Morgan placed his best foot soldiers. Out of sight, lower down on the other hill, he stationed Colonel Washington's cavalry. In reserve was the main body of militia troops.

On came the dashing Tarleton, always in haste. For two days he had been chasing Morgan. He arrived at the Cowpens with his men and horses fatigued from an all-night ride. Morgan's force had had some rest. And breakfast, too.

Almost any commander except Colonel Tarleton would have given his men and animals a breathing spell and food before going into action. But he was the sort, as Morgan well knew, who simply could not delay action when chance offered him some. Morgan's troops on the hill could see the Dragoons' commander as he rode to and fro before his troops, pointing with his sword to where the Americans were stationed. Tarleton's trumpeters blew the signal, and his tired if willing command went charging up the hill.

Morgan's men were waiting. Minutes before the British were ready to charge, he had told his first line of foot soldiers what to do. "All I want from you," he said, "is two shots apiece—two volleys.

"And don't shoot at all until they are in killing distance," he warned. "Just two volleys at fifty yards. Then you can drop back."

Morgan's men remembered. With young John Eager Howard in command of their line, they held their fire as the green wave of Dragoons came pounding up the hill. Then they loosed the first shattering volley. Fifteen of Tarleton's horsemen went tumbling. The animals reared and screamed. The green wave was halted. The unhorsed survivors slashed about with their sabers. Then the Americans fired again, and withdrew.

Hand-to-hand fighting continued, and the Royal artillery at the base of the first hill began belching as the American militia reserve came in, Colonel Andrew Pickens leading them through the grapeshot that was falling like rain. The green-clad Dragoons broke at last. In another moment they were reeling down the hill.

Before the Americans had time to cheer, they heard the skirling of bagpipes, and up came the 71st Highlanders in perfect formation, to attack from the flank. Young John Howard ordered a company of militia to wheel to the left, in order to face the 71st. The order was misunderstood. The militia turned and marched, still in good order, *to the rear.*

It looked like a retreat. General Morgan saw it and came riding to stem matters before panic could set in.

Colonel Tarleton also saw it. To him it looked as

Morgan's men remembered his orders: "Just two

volleys at fifty yards. Then you can drop back."

if victory was in his hands. He ordered another charge.

Just then Colonel William Washington's horsemen came thundering up from their hiding place beyond the second hill, hitting the British with terrific impact.

Though the Royal artillery continued to roar and smoke and to pelt the hill, the British lines were broken and in complete confusion. In another few moments, redcoats and green coats were throwing down their arms. Others were riding or fleeing on foot to the rear.

The Americans did not let up pressure. With a few of his horsemen, Colonel Washington charged the fifty-odd green Dragoons who were retreating with Tarleton himself. Tarleton turned back in defiance, rising in his stirrups and aiming a saber stroke at Washington, who parried the blow with a broken sword. Tarleton then drew his pistol and fired. The shot missed Washington by a hair and wounded his horse. Tarleton then turned to dash after his fleeing Dragoons.

It was the end of the Battle of the Cowpens. In a

little less than an hour's fighting, the British had met their worst disaster since Saratoga. They suffered 100 dead, 39 of them officers. On the field they also left 229 wounded, and 600 prisoners. They lost two cannons, 100 good horses, 36 wagons, and one stand of colors.

The Americans lost twelve killed, and sixty wounded.

That night the defeated Dragoons camped after crossing the Broad River. "In his anguish over the loss of his troops," so wrote Tarleton's biographer, Robert D. Bass, "Colonel Tarleton cast himself upon the cold, wet ground and lay open-eyed through the wintry night."

Next day Tarleton rode into Cornwallis's camp about twenty-five miles from the Cowpens to report what must have seemed to his lordship an almost incredible defeat.

Cowpens changed everything Cornwallis had been planning. It had come just when the British commander was preparing to advance triumphantly toward the heart of North Carolina, believing he had subdued South Carolina beyond recovery. Tarleton's disaster withered that idea. "It almost broke my heart," Cornwallis confided to a brother officer.

Surveying the scene, it seemed to the British commander that his hope now was the destruction of Greene's entire army. He could begin by destroying Dan Morgan.

Five days after Cowpens General Nathanael Greene got the news. Elated though he was, this was no time to celebrate, to break out a victory ration of rum for the troops. He must follow up the astonishing success of General Morgan.

So, issuing a whole raft of orders, delegating responsibilities and actions to be taken, Greene set out overland with a small detail of hard-riding horsemen to find Morgan. It was to be a wild and reckless dash through enemy country.

Greene's orders: General Isaac Huger and such troops as he could put in marching order were to start north at once toward the Dan River in North Carolina and Virginia.

Quartermaster Edward Carrington must ride ahead of Huger. When he got to the Dan he was to collect every boat and scow that would float, and set civilians to building more boats.

Light-Horse Harry Lee's Legion must be withdrawn immediately from service with General Marion, and join the main army under Greene (or Huger).

General Marion was to continue to make trouble on Cornwallis's supply lines inland from the coast. He was to raid such supplies as possible and send them to Greene's army. Marion must also watch for expected Tory musters and break them up.

The news of Cowpens came to Snow Island as Marion and Lee were preparing another raid on Georgetown. Now this must be called off. With the dispatch came orders that Lee and his Legion should ride to join Greene's army as soon as possible.

It was with genuine regret that the Swamp Fox bade farewell to Light-Horse Harry. They had got along famously. "I know we shall meet again," Colonel Lee said, as Marion personally guided him and the Legion through the Snow Island swamps and put them on the road north.

·VI·

THE CHASE OF
COLONEL WATSON

In his camp on Snow Island Marion considered the
orders he had received from his commander. The
sudden departure of Lee and his Legion had left the
brigade with too few men to attempt to attack Georgetown again. But if General Greene wanted him to
harass the British supply lines out of Georgetown and
Charleston, well, that was another matter. He could
still make war Indian-style—hit and run.

Calling his trusted Major John Postell, General
Marion suggested an immediate attack on the enemy.

"Take twenty-five of your best horsemen," he told the major. "And be prepared to leave here tonight."

"Where to?"

"Wadboo Bridge. A scout just came in to report that a sizeable wagon train of supplies is stopping there to make some repairs."

"What about guards?" the Major asked.

"The scout wasn't sure, but he didn't see more than a squad or two of men besides the teamsters. I think your twenty-five horsemen can handle them without trouble."

"Yes, sir."

"Hit 'em before daylight," General Marion ordered. "Set the wagons afire, then get out of there quickly, and ride for Moncks Corner."

"Anything to do at the Corner?" the Major wanted to know.

"I hope so. By the time you get to the Corner another supply train should be at that place, stopping to feed the horses. If so, see what you can do."

Major Postell and his horsemen performed beautifully. The double-goaled raid came off without a hitch. Almost before the few guards knew what had struck them, the wagon train at Wadboo Bridge was in flames, and Postell and his troop were yelling to stampede the train's horses as they rode away for Moncks Corner.

They struck the Corner at a dead run, shooting down guards, then surrounded the long train of eleven wagons just as daylight was breaking. Without another shot, Postell's men took thirty-five prisoners. The wagons turned out to be loaded with clothing and blankets but no ammunition.

Because it was General Marion's declared policy to parole all prisoners as soon as they were captured, Major Postell did so with the British guards and wagoners at Moncks Corner. Then, after taking as much clothing and blankets as his men could carry on horseback, Postell ordered the wagons and their contents set on fire. Only after that was done did he ride away from the Corner through the smoke of supplies that were never to reach Cornwallis.

General Marion was highly pleased that the double raid had not cost him a man. On the other hand, he was disappointed that it had not solved his worst problem: His brigade had no more than two rounds

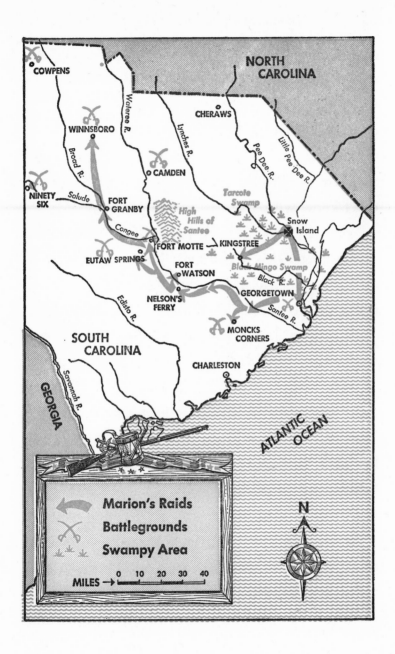

NORTH CAROLINA

COWPENS

CHERAWS

WINNSBORO

Wateree R.

Lynches R.

Pee Dee R.

Little Pee Dee R.

Broad R.

CAMDEN

NINETY SIX

Salude

FORT GRANBY

Congee

Tarcote Swamp

High Hills of Santee

Snow Island

FORT MOTTE — KINGSTREE

EUTAW SPRINGS

FORT WATSON

Black Mingo Swamp

Black R.

GEORGETOWN

NELSON'S FERRY

Santee R.

SOUTH CAROLINA

Edisto R.

MONCKS CORNERS

CHARLESTON

GEORGIA

Savannah R.

ATLANTIC OCEAN

N

Marion's Raids

Battlegrounds

Swampy Area

MILES →   0   10   20   30   40

of powder-and-shot per man. Something must be
done, and at once. Major Postell and his brave raiders
were still enjoying a belated breakfast when Marion
called Colonel Peter Horry to his tent.

"Colonel, not one ounce of powder came from
those twenty British wagons," Marion said. "And I
don't know where we can find any."

"We were promised one keg by General Greene's
quartermaster two weeks ago," Horry replied.

"Send a rider to him. Say that Marion's brigade is
down to two rounds."

"If *that* much," said Horry, adding, "I doubt that
we have two rounds."

"While we are waiting for that keg," said the General, "we can do something, at least for our cavalry."
Then he dispatched Horry and a detail to collect all
the saws they could find at mills, plantations and
farms along the Mingo and Black rivers. "Take them
to Kingstree," said the General. "I'll be waiting there."

As Horry's men came in to the little village in
small groups, bringing old saws, new saws, broken
saws, they found that General Marion had been recruiting all the professional and amateur blacksmiths

in the neighborhood. Charcoal fires were quickly lighted in every shop. Young boys swung happily on the long handles and pumped the great bellows that made the saw-metal glow red.

Then the brawny smiths went clamorously to work, hammer on anvil, to forge the steel. In showers of pretty sparks, the saws soon took on the shape of broadswords, and were doused, still spitting fire, to cool and steam in the water tubs.

If Marion's men could get no powder and ball, they could go into battle, if they must, with the weapons of primitive men. Within another two weeks some of them did so.

The occasion was a sudden attack staged by the brigade on a supply train which had stopped to rest and feed at Nelson's Ferry on the way to the British fort at Ninety-Six. The train was guarded by some two hundred foot soldiers in command of a Major MacIlraith.

Taking his position twenty-five miles from the Ferry, Marion placed his men carefully. It was to be an ambush. Letting the wagon column rumble past, Marion sent Horry and his horsemen to attack the rear guard. Armed with one round each and their new broadswords, Horry's troop killed or wounded several of the British, and panicked the rest.

Marion meanwhile was leading the main command roundabout through the timber, to set up another ambush a few miles ahead. This time both the advance and the rearguards were hit, and a number of soldiers killed. So far, not one of Marion's men had been wounded.

A brave if conventional soldier, Major MacIlraith had had enough of this Indian-style fighting. He moved his column into an open field, and set his men in position for a formal battle, the sort he and they were used to. But then he changed his mind. Sending one of his officers under a flag of truce, MacIlraith made as strange a proposal to Marion as could be imagined.

It was more like something out of the days of knights-in-armor than anything else. Here, according to eyewitnesses and set down in quaint style in Lossing's old *Field-Book of the American Revolution,* was what happened:

"Both sides had prepared for battle when Mac-

Saws soon took on the shape of broadswords.

Ilraith, who was a most humane man, made the chiv-
alric proposition that twenty picked men of each
army should meet and fight for victory. It was agreed
to. The forty men were drawn up in line and approached each other, when those of MacIlraith's party
fell back. The sun went down, and yet they lingered;
and at midnight MacIlraith, doubtless considering
prudence the better part of valor, decamped, leaving
his heavy baggage behind. He was pursued by Colonel Horry early in the morning, but without effect."

Incredible though it seems today, MacIlraith's proposition may have been a wild ruse to get him out of
a tight spot. He had no horse soldiers to put against
Marion's mounted men. He was encumbered with
tons of supplies. He had already experienced the
deadly hit-and-run tactics of Marion's men. His odd
proposal delayed further action that day by the Americans. After dark, he piled his campfires high with
wood to last through the night, then, as the old account has it, he "decamped, leaving his heavy baggage behind."

The heavy baggage was of course the British supplies, and these Marion was more than glad to take.

Most of this material consisted of provisions intended for Ninety-Six. And though the record is not clear, search of the wagons seems to have rewarded the Americans with an extremely small amount of powder.

Detailing teamsters and guards to take the train eastward to the Pee Dee River, then up that stream to General Greene's receiving depot in the Cheraws region, Marion and the rest of the brigade returned to headquarters on Snow Island.

It will be recalled that General Nathanael Greene had long since moved his main army north to the Dan River region. Cornwallis had moved north, too, hoping to catch and demolish Greene, meanwhile leaving the British command in South Carolina to young Lord Rawdon, son of an Irish peer.

Now, Rawdon needed, if for no other reason than to make a reputation, to accomplish something important while Cornwallis was away. What could be more important than to wipe out the troublesome Marion and his tough backwoodsmen? Nothing. So now Rawdon sent Colonel Watson with a British regiment, and Harrison's brigade of Tories, amounting in all to some five hundred men, plus two pieces of artillery, with orders to put an end to Marion's raiding.

When word of this plan reached Marion, he set out from Snow Island, with all the men he could muster, to meet Watson.

What Marion did not know at this time was that Rawdon had also dispatched another British regiment, under Colonel Doyle, with similar orders to those given Colonel Watson: do away with Marion. Doyle's orders suggested that he begin his campaign by following down Lynchs Creek and meeting Watson on the Pee Dee.

Marion found Watson's forces in a swamp not far from Nelson's Ferry on the Santee. Action began at once when Colonel Peter Horry's advance guard ran into a detachment of Watson's cavalry. Watson immediately unlimbered his guns on a rise of ground and drove Horry from the swamp, then sent Tory horsemen led by Major Harrison to attack him.

Horry's troop was forced into a rearguard action against superior numbers, and might well have been wiped out had not Marion at that moment sent in his cavalry under young Captain Daniel Conyers. Though Conyers had been under fire before, this was the first time he had commanded troops in a battle. Breaking away from his own men, and slashing a road through the Tory horsemen, he attacked the veteran Major Harrison, and killed him with his sword.

In this action Marion's brigade did so much damage that Watson, protected by his artillery, went into camp on Cantey's plantation and remained in a state of siege for nearly a week. Meanwhile the brigade watched and waited for a move.

When Watson at last moved again, Marion acted as though he were retreating in front of the British advance. But only for a few miles. Then, while Watson was keeping a close eye on the Swamp Fox, Colonel Horry again hit the redcoats, and ran. So did Major James's horsemen, who also rode ahead and tore up a bridge in advance of the British.

There was more hot action here at the wrecked bridge. When Watson sent men to repair the structure, James's sharpshooters opened fire from the woods, and work halted until Watson could wheel up his artillery. But the muzzles of the guns could not be depressed sufficiently to get the sharpshooters within range. As soon as this became apparent, James's riflemen were back at their sport of picking off the cannoneers. Watson gave up the bridge as bad business. He would ford the river.

But Captain Conyers was ahead of him. When Watson's advance guard came down to the ford, and just as they reached the water, Conyers's boys opened fire at a hundred yards and to terrible effect.

Colonel Watson decided to stay on his own side, and to move upriver to Blakeley's plantation. Here he pitched camp. And here he stayed for ten days, inactive, watched by Marion's brigade.

Watson was getting desperate. Even in camp, his men were targets for Marion's riflemen concealed in the woods. Presently a British officer approached Marion's position with a white flag. Colonel Watson wished permission to send some of his badly wounded to Georgetown, where they could get the care they needed. General Marion gladly granted permission to "Lieut. Torriano and six wounded men, with six privates to attend them," to pass unmolested through the American lines.

A day later Colonel Watson hastily broke camp, and just as hastily took off down the Santee road, with Horry's troops hanging on one flank, taking pot shots every little while. Marion attacked the rear when chance offered. The running battle continued until Sampit Bridge was reached, only nine miles from Georgetown. There the brigade left their quarry, including two wagonloads of wounded, to stagger on into the British-held town.

Why their General had suddenly given up the chase, instead of harrying the enemy until he reached his stone barracks, must have seemed a deep mystery to Marion's men. During the excitement of the galloping battle, few of them would have noticed a messenger on a horse white with lather who rode up to General Marion and handed him a note. It was brief, one line:

"Snow Island camp demolished by Doyle's regiment."

And it was a shocker. It was also almost beyond belief. Tarleton hadn't been able to find the Snow Is-

land hide-out. Neither had other British officers.
Who was Doyle and what was his regiment? Until
now Marion had never heard of Doyle. The little
general was worried. He shouted to Colonel Horry.
"Call off the fight!" he cried. Then, as Major James

The wounded British soldiers were sent to Georgetown.

came up, he asked that officer to inform Horry to
bring the brigade back to Lynchs Creek as soon as
possible. "I'm going there now," Marion said, slap-
ping his horse, and away he went up the road.

·VII·

MARION'S HIDE-OUT
IS DISCOVERED

Ball, the faithful sorrel horse, felt the urgency of his master. Taking off from Sampit Bridge like a hound after a rabbit, he hardly slowed his pace until General Marion drew up at a farmhouse on the bank of Lynchs Creek not far from Snow Island.

The aged farmer was in the yard. Marion knew him as the father of two sons serving in the brigade. "Seen any redcoats around here?" Marion asked.

"Yes, sir, General, the road was full of 'em this morning, but they was heading north."

"How many?"

"I don't just know," the farmer answered. "But there must have been hundreds."

"How long since?"

"Four, maybe six hours."

"Make you any trouble?" General Marion asked.

"No, sir. They was in a tear. I heard the officers yelling, hurrying them up."

"Any idea where they were going?"

"Yes, sir, I have. A couple of them stopped to get a drink of water. They was grumbling. Had to march here all the way from Camden. Now they got here, they got to march right back to Camden again. No sense, the way they figured it."

Well, that was that. It was too late to catch Doyle's regiment. Though Marion could only guess why they had gone back to Camden on the double-quick, the four or more hours' start made it futile to try to catch them—even if the brigade were here and ready, which it wasn't.

Marion thanked the old farmer, and was riding on toward Snow Island when a man with a musket appeared in the road. It was one of Marion's own soldiers, one of the handful of guards who had been left at the hide-out camp. "General," he said, "there ain't no need to go further. Them redcoats didn't leave nothing at the Island."

Marion got down to let Ball rest, and listened to the sorrowful guard's account of what happened at Snow Island. Early that morning a large body of British regulars had appeared at the brigade's camp. They had been guided through the swamps by a Tory farmer of the neighborhood.

Except for Colonel John Ervin and four men, the camp was deserted. The redcoat officers were amazed to find that this notorious camp of the Swamp Fox contained no barracks or houses of any sort, save for a crude shelter for food and other stores, numerous lean-tos and a number of ragged tents.

The British commander, Colonel Doyle, was shocked. "Is *this* the headquarters of General Marion?" he cried. "Marion who has caused us so much trouble?" It did not seem possible.

The redcoats were not long in collecting the odd assortment of old muskets, pistols, and swords, together with the salt meat and sweet potatoes that comprised the brigade's commissary, and dumping them into the black, deep waters of the creek. Then Doyle and his party left Snow Island to rejoin their regiment.

The destruction of the headquarters hide-out must have saddened General Marion. The place had served him well. It had served the United States well, too, though few Americans had yet heard of it. And how much Snow Island had cost the British was not to be calculated.

No use to weep. Anyway, there was no time to weep. Things were about to move swiftly.

Within another hour or so along came Colonel Horry and the brigade, all the men tired, some of them bloody from the brisk fight at Sampit Bridge. Marion halted them on the road and told them what had happened to Snow Island. "We'll go into camp right here," he said.

Before morning a scout came looking for General Marion. Doyle and his regiment, said the scout, were making a forced march to Camden on orders received from Lord Rawdon, now commanding the British army in South Carolina. The sudden haste, so rumor

The guard told Marion what had happened at Snow Island.

had it, was due to the fact that General Nathanael Greene had fought a battle with Cornwallis at Guilford Court House, up in North Carolina, and was moving south.

Marion and his men had not moved from their temporary camp when another scout came in, this time to report that British Colonel Watson was on the march again. After being driven by the brigade into Georgetown, he had got reinforcements, was freshly supplied with arms, ammunition and supplies, and was now moving back into the Pee Dee district. Not only that; he was already *there,* and going into camp on Fish Creek not more than five miles distant.

Marion called Colonel Horry to learn just how much powder and ball was left in the brigade.

"Not one shot more than two rounds per man," Horry said.

"That settles it," said Marion. "We can't make war on Watson and his five hundred men with two shots apiece." He thought a moment, sipping his vinegar water. "Colonel," he went on, "call our boys together. Tell them they might better go home than to wait here. Watson surely will find us in a day or so. Perhaps he knows where we are already. We can't make war without powder. Our men have plowing to do, and other farm work. Spring is almost here."

"Yes, sir. Better disperse before Watson learns where we are."

"Horry, tell the boys we will let them know when we can be soldiers again."

Horry explained the sorry conditions to the brigade. In pairs and small groups, the men began leaving camp. The officers, though, had talked matters over and decided they should stick with their general.

But what to do? This was the subject being discussed when an aged farmer, Baker Johnson, came wandering into camp, weary and half starved. "Give me something to eat," he told Gavin Witherspoon, one of Marion's youngest captains. "Ain't had a meal in two days."

Sharing a bowl of rice with the old fellow, Witherspoon got him to talking. Soon Johnson was babbling something about "Continental troops." It didn't make sense to the young officer, but he decided he might as well humor the elderly man, let him talk. "*What* Continental troops?" he asked.

"I don't know who they are," Johnson replied, "but I see them with my own eyes, fair as could be. They was passing Long Bluff. Soldiers, I tell you! Horse and foot. Lots of 'em."

Witherspoon was listening now. "Come with me," he said, "and tell General Marion."

"I will not," the old man replied. "Let the General

come to me. I am eating my first meal in three days."

Witherspoon went to tell Marion. "I know old Johnson," the General said. "He is a dependable man. I will go to him." Johnson repeated his story. He was still talking and eating when a sudden rattle as if from drums broke the forest quiet. It was startling. Marion turned to face the direction of the noise. Where were his pickets? Had they fallen asleep?

Not quite. Above the drumming came the shout

"We have only two rounds per man," Horry told Marion.

of challenge. In another moment Marion and his men watched spellbound as a small troop of smart horsemen came riding into the clearing, a mounted drummer beating the march.

The leading trooper halted his men, then dismounted and came to Marion. "Sir," said he with a salute, "Colonel Harry Lee presents his compliments to General Marion, and says he will arrive tonight with his Legion."

If Marion and his soldiers were astonished almost beyond words, old Baker Johnson wasn't. He was delighted. "See!" he crowed. "See! I told you they was Continentals passing Long Bluff. And I told you right and true!"

So he had. Late that evening Light-Horse Harry and his Legion, four hundred strong, arrived at Marion's camp. They were made welcome by what the Swamp Fox declared, with some humor, to be a "modest feast for tired soldiers." The feast comprised sweet potatoes baked in hot ashes, some boiled beef with a little salt, and a strange mixture of roasted grain called coffee.

While the new arrivals feasted and talked with the

few of Marion's privates still in camp, Marion and his officers listened intently while Colonel Lee related what had been going on in Virginia and North Carolina.

After the British defeat at Cowpens by Dan Morgan, Cornwallis decided that his next move was to catch and destroy Morgan, then catch and destroy General Greene. But he would have to move fast, for both wings of the American force had already started north.

Cornwallis meant business. Stripping his army, he spent two days burning his wagons and stores, including tents and all provisions except what the men could carry in their knapsacks. He even had the heads of all rum casks staved in. This so disgusted the Hessians that more than two hundred of them deserted.

Cornwallis now had an army peeled down to absolute necessities and able to move rapidly. On the last day of January (1781) he set out, with two thousand troops, to catch Morgan. If he could not bring either Morgan or Greene into open action, then he would strike for the Dan River, watching the fords and ferries. British scouts had told him that the Dan could not be forded at this time of year. If he could drive the Americans against the Dan quickly, and catch them on the south bank, the Dan would be their death trap.

What the British commander did not know was that Greene had already sent his quartermaster to collect all available boats on the Dan and to have them ready. Cornwallis did not learn of this move until he and his army reached the swollen river. Then they found that all the boats were on the opposite bank. And so was General Greene.

Weeks passed, and while Cornwallis fumed and raided south of the Dan, Greene recruited soldiers from the training camps being operated in Virginia by the great drillmaster, Baron von Steuben.

Though rheumatism had at last forced Colonel Daniel Morgan to retire, his troops were in command of Ortho Williams, the young Marylander General Greene had appointed his adjutant general. Greene also had Colonel William Washington with him, and Colonel Lee and his Legion. By late February Greene took stock of his army. On paper it showed up as some four thousand men, though the quality of many of them was as yet untried. Still, Greene thought he was strong enough to recross the Dan.

Once that was done, General Greene's plan was to move his troops directly toward Cornwallis's main army, as if he meant to attack, and then to halt suddenly at a spot he had previously selected with great care. Green hoped this spot would serve as a decoy to attract the British commander into attacking the Americans.

The place chosen by Greene to give battle was a tiny hamlet on the map of North Carolina called Guilford Court House. And there, sure enough, on March 15, Cornwallis attacked.

The battle went into history as a British victory. Greene, after a brief and bloody fight, retreated. Cornwallis remained upon the field. The British had, however, suffered much the greater loss. As historian Bruce Lancaster summed it up: "General Greene had perhaps lost a battle but he had won a campaign."

After Guilford Court House, Greene started at once to move back to South Carolina. Cornwallis made no move to stop him. Instead, he retired to the

North Carolina port of Wilmington to care for his
many wounded and to refit his command. He was
never to move south again. When he did move, a little later, it was north to the Yorktown Peninsula of
Virginia, a place he was to help to make famous. For
it was here that the last battle of the Revolution was
fought.

One of the last things General Greene did before
he struck out to return south was to send Colonel
Lee and his Legion to report to General Marion.

Here they were now, and Marion presently received a message from Greene suggesting two targets
for immediate attention. These were the British posts
named Fort Watson and Fort Motte.

·VIII·

THE BRIGADE TAKES
FORT WATSON

It was clear enough to Marion and Lee why General Greene wanted them to knock out the two forts. They stood guard on Lord Rawdon's line of communications and supply between Camden and the ports of Georgetown and Charleston. And Greene meant to bring Rawdon to battle.

Fort Watson was more than a guardpost; in it was a large warehouse which a spy from Marion's brigade said was filled with British arms, ammunition and provisions. That alone made it worth-while to take.

Neither Marion nor Lee were men to dodge a raid.

On the very afternoon they met, their troops began moving toward Fort Watson. Marion meanwhile sent couriers to recall his soldiers whom he had sent home because of the lack of ammunition.

Fort Watson turned out to be no place for a hit-and-run raid. Neither was it to be taken by a head-long charge. It stood on top of an ancient Indian mound, rising forty feet above the surface of Scott's Lake, which was really a wide spot of the Santee River a few miles above Nelson's Ferry.

The ground leading up to the well-built stockade was very steep. There were three lines of felled and sharpened trees—a forerunner of barbed-wire—to be penetrated on the way up the hill. No, it would never do to charge this bastion without artillery. Marion and Lee had no artillery. After one look at Fort Watson, Marion dispatched a horseman to General Greene asking for a field gun with which to bombard the fort.

All timber and brush within musket-shot of the stockade had been cleared away, a fact made clear when Marion and Lee rode too near the fort. Bullets from redcoats plowed the ground near them.

Within the fort was Lieutenant McKay, a brave young officer of the British Regular Army, in command of one hundred and twenty soldiers. To him General Marion now sent a man under a flag of truce, demanding immediate surrender of the garrison. McKay refused. He doubtless expected the approach any moment of Colonel Watson and his large force —not knowing that British officer had retired to Georgetown.

When surrender was refused, Marion turned his attention to the fort's water supply. Cut that off, and the besieged must give in. American sharpshooters were placed where their bullets could command the river by the fort and prevent water from that source.

But Lieutenant McKay was not giving in so easily. He set his men to digging within the stockade. And though it was a long way down to reach the water level, within another two days the British were drinking fresh water from the deep well. Lee and Marion must try something else.

No word had come from General Greene, and no gun, either. The American attack was stalled. How long this inactivity might have lasted is anybody's guess; but at this point one of Marion's officers came forward to suggest an ingenious method of attack.

Give him a smart crew of axmen, said Major Hezekiah Maham, and during one night he would raise a tower high enough for riflemen to shoot into the fort.

Here was a really bold idea. Because the tower must be built within gunshot of the fort, it would have to be erected between dark and dawn. And quietly, too, lest the British know what was going on and begin shooting blindly into the dark. Marion and Lee realized the difficulties. They may not have been convinced the tower could be put up during the hours of darkness without raising the suspicions of Lieutenant McKay.

Yet, what else could be done? Wait for the cannon from General Greene? Valuable time had already been lost. There was no sign of artillery. "Major," said Marion to Maham, "take such men as you can use, and go ahead. Issue your orders."

Major Maham knew exactly what he needed first —all the axes he could get. Forming six small details of horsemen, each in charge of an officer, he sent them up the Santee, down the Santee, and ranging east and west from that river.

"Call at every plantation," he instructed them. "Call at every mill, every farmhouse, every cabin. Beg or buy, or simply take if you must, every ax you can lay hands on."

Away they went in every direction. Maham now set men to locating such cutting tools as were to be found in the brigade. Then he asked for volunteers from among soldiers who were expert woodcutters, men familiar with the felling of trees. At least half a hundred stepped forth, twice as many as there were axes in the command.

"Come with me," said Major Maham, and followed by twenty-odd men with axes on their shoulders, and another fifty ready to take their turn at chopping or any other work, he led them back into thick woods more than a quarter of a mile from the fort.

Maham let his experienced eye sweep the forest, then selected a slim, tall pine, straight as an arrow. "Men," said he, "this is the kind we want. It is perfect for our purpose. It will make at least four logs each twelve feet long. Here," he spoke to a couple of the volunteers, "show me what you can do."

The two rugged young men stepped up to the base of the pine, spat on their hands and, without a word, set to work to make the undercut. Like clockwork the axes rose and fell, thudding into the trunk while chips as big as plates flew through the air like bullets.

These were real woodsmen! When the first cut was well into the heartwood, the two men, again without a word or sign, suddenly shifted position to the opposite side of the tree, then began chopping a few inches higher than the undercut. In another few moments the tall pine was seen to shiver, to lean, then to crash to the ground.

The tree had little more than hit the ground before four more axmen swarmed all over it, cutting off the limbs, then the top—and *there* lay a good forty-eight feet of pine on the forest floor. In a jiffy, the axmen cut it into logs of about equal length.

No sooner were the clean logs ready than they were each lifted on the shoulders of two strong fellows, or carried on a bed of stout poles, like a litter, by a dozen men. And off they went almost to the edge of the clearing nearest the fort, and left in neat piles—called "landings" by woodsmen—from which they could easily be picked up when the time came.

Major Maham was delighted by the manner in which these soldiers went at their task. Virtually all of them had used axes since they were big enough to chop, and now they vied with one another. Chips were flying and axes thudding, and there was a stop only for a brief moment as another pine fell. Then came the different sound of limbs being cut, the swish of pine branches, and at last the heave-ho and grunts of the men acting in place of horses, which could not be used because of lack of harness and chains.

Long before noon the first details of ax-gatherers returned to report to Major Maham, and at once another twenty choppers went to work with the new tools. Maham himself was everywhere, seeing that the best choppers were spelled off occasionally by changing the work-details which were taking the sticks to the landings.

Dinnertime was staggered in order that there should be no halt in the logging. While some sat down to corn bread and tea, others kept the chips flying. By mid-afternoon another two dozen axes had come. Suppertime and early twilight found the landings piled head-high and more with the neat, straight logs. Major Maham detailed two veteran woodsmen to count the sticks, then with a pencil he figured on a clean new stump how many more were needed to raise the tower high enough to command the interior of Fort Watson.

(In Fort Watson that day, Lieutenant McKay and his soldiers grew curious at the medley of noise that came to them vaguely from back in the timber. They could see nothing at all. What could the Americans be up to? The British could guess, and that is all they could do. And they were guessing wrong all the time.)

As the first shadows of night fell over the forest, the choppers and the beasts-of-burden of Maham's crew were ordered to rest for the supreme effort ahead.

During the daylight hours, Major Maham had selected the place where the tower should rise. Now he went about in the twilight checking the logs, marking the paths the men should follow out of the woods, and selecting the officers who should lead the work parties of the night. He also sought out the six sharp-shooting members of his own company in the brigade who, come daylight, were to have the posts of honor and of danger in the attack on the fort.

"Now, my boys," he said, "look well to your guns. If they are not in perfect working order, go to the quartermaster and get guns that are."

"Yes, sir."

"Look to your horns. See that they are filled to the tip."

"Yes, sir."

"With *dry* powder," the Major insisted. "Above all, check your flints. Then go to bed. I'll call you when the time comes."

To their blankets went the six sharpshooters, while throughout the very early morning hours Maham's crew worked like shadows. Log upon log, crisscross, the tower rose steadily—ten feet, twenty feet, thirty feet. With men spaced a few feet apart, hanging to the wall like firemen to a ladder, the smaller sticks went upward hand over hand.

Forty feet. Maham himself climbed up. "We want another few rounds of logs," he told the men at the top, and he stayed while the needed sticks came up and were laid.

"Now for the parapet, the protection," Maham said. Up came more logs, to be piled solid except for notches that had already been made for rifle portholes.

It was a little after four o'clock. All was ready for the sharpshooters when daylight came. Maham and the others came down to the ground. He sent orderlies to awaken the riflemen. He even inspected their arms, their powder horns, and checked their bullets. Then he gave them final orders.

"Lie flat on the tower," he said. "Let two of you act as lookouts to keep an eye on the fort. I can give you but one rule about shooting. Shoot instantly when you see the first redcoat moving inside the stockade. And not until then. Keep on shooting. Don't stop until I shout. I'll be right here in this clump of bushes," he went on, indicating the spot where they were talking. "You will be able to hear me."

The six riflemen said they understood the orders, then they climbed slowly and carefully to the top of the tower and lay down behind the parapet. The night wore on. The sky gradually turned to gray. Maham was at his post in the bushes. General Marion and Colonel Lee stood nearby, waiting. So did most of the brigade. This was no time to sleep.

Up at the tower top six pairs of sharp eyes were glued on the interior of Fort Watson. The tips of six rifle barrels protruded a few inches through the portholes. Six trigger fingers were ready to crook.

To the waiting marksmen, peering through the portholes, it was like seeing a peep show. The stage was Fort Watson as seen from above. And as gray dawn turned lighter, out from the main barracks inside the stockade came an actor—a figure in a coat of bright red, a wonderful target.

Up in the tower one finger squeezed. Flame and smoke puffed from a porthole. A lead ball whistled past an ear of the lone redcoat and thudded into the wall behind him. There he stood for a moment, shocked with astonishment.

Another porthole flamed, and the British soldier

Four of the tower riflemen picked a target.

was knocked backward against the wall. The bullet had caught him in the shoulder. He shouted. An instant later the fort's parade ground was alive with running figures.

Four of the tower riflemen picked a target and pulled the trigger. Two redcoats went tumbling to the ground. The others ran back into the barrack. The riflemen reloaded. Down on the ground in the rear of the tower, General Marion spoke to Maham. "Major," he asked, "may I send my men in now?"

"Yes, sir. Send them in. The boys on the tower will try to cover them."

Marion gave the order, and out of the woods came the detail of volunteers formed during the night; ten of Marion's brigade, ten of Lee's Legion. They streaked across the open ground like so many deer. Axes in hand, they attacked what Marion had guessed to be the weakest spot of the stockade.

The British saw them coming. And the men in the tower saw redcoats start running to the danger spot. Again the tower portholes breathed flame and smoke. A redcoat was seen to throw up his arms and go down. Two more were hit, then dropped their guns. But half a dozen brave British soldiers reached the stockade just as the Americans were about to enter and let go a volley of pistol fire at close range.

Smoke obscured the melee at the stockade. The instant it began to clear, the tower boys fired. The redcoats, several of them wounded, turned to run for cover.

At this moment, too, General Marion sent the entire brigade forward to charge up the hill and enter the fort through the breach. Before they had moved halfway, a white flag appeared above the stockade. Marion called to his men. The fire from the tower ceased.

Lieutenant McKay, Fort Watson's commander, knew the battle was lost. A few minutes later he came out to meet General Marion and formally surrender. His garrison troops numbered one hundred and twenty men and officers, less six killed and twice as many wounded.

Due to the ingenuity of Major Hezekiah Maham, Fort Watson had been taken by the Americans with a loss of only two killed and six wounded.

Following his usual custom, General Marion paroled all of the prisoners on their oath they would not again bear arms against the Americans.

The fruits of victory were more than prisoners. The warehouse in Fort Watson was filled to the doors with things the Americans needed: Blankets, muskets, keg after keg of powder, hundreds of pounds of bullets, a whole barrel of flints, even a score of bright bayonets; to say nothing of salted meats, corn, corn meal, potatoes, hardtack, and a stock of tea.

In a brief letter to General Greene, Marion reported the fall of Fort Watson and the capture of its garrison and supplies. Though always a man of few words, it was typical of the Swamp Fox to take pains to cite Major Maham as the officer chiefly responsible for the reduction of the fort.

Then, while their men feasted on the British rations, and the powder and other supplies were being distributed and wagonloads of provisions started on their way to Greene's camp, Marion and Lee began preparations to attack the other British post Greene had mentioned. This was Fort Motte.

· IX ·

FORT MOTTE PROVES TOUGH

General Marion already had a pretty good idea of
what Fort Motte was like. Even while he and Lee
were besieging Fort Watson, one of Marion's spies,
in the guise of a Tory, had visited the other fort and
returned with an excellent description of it.

It stood on a high rolling plain on the plantation
of Mrs. Rebecca Motte, a widow and mother of six
children, near the junction of the Congaree and the
Wateree rivers, less than a day's march from Fort
Watson. When the British decided to have a fort

there, they had evicted Mrs. Motte, her family and
her house slaves from the great mansion and moved
them into quarters of the plantation overseer half a
mile to the north. This was a small farmhouse. There
were also several cabins for the field hands.

Taking over the fine mansion for his headquarters,
Captain MacPherson, the British commander, set his
men to building a stockade of immense logs around
the camp and to digging a deep, broad ditch around
the stockade. With such defenses, added to its natural position on high ground, the post now commanded everything within gunshot.

Marion's spy, a thorough man, also reported that
within the stockade was a deep well capable of sup-
plying all the water needed by the one hundred and
sixty-five soldiers of MacPherson's garrison. What
was more, said the spy, the British had dug a trench
from the mansion to the well for the protection of
the men while procuring water.

Marion complimented the alert spy for keeping
his eyes open, but he wanted to know one more thing.
"Did you notice," he asked, "if the British have any
artillery?"

"Sir, I saw no sign of field guns."

"Did you notice anything that looked like preparation for a battery?"

"No, sir, I did not."

This was good news. While their troops were getting ready for the march north to Fort Motte, Marion and Lee were cheered when a Major Eaton and squad of gunners arrived to join them with a small cannon, a six-pounder. General Greene had sent gun and men too late for the attack on Fort Watson. Perhaps they could use it on the other fort.

General Marion led his little command past Fort Motte at some distance, and arrived at Mrs. Motte's temporary home in the farmhouse half a mile north of the fortified mansion. The vivacious and brilliant widow greeted the Americans joyfully, setting a table with tea and cakes for General Marion and Colonel Lee with such style as she could command under the circumstances.

Crowded as she and her family were in the small farmhouse, she announced nevertheless that the two officers must make it their headquarters. She would move into one of the cabins. Marion and Lee would not hear of it. They soon joined their troops camped around in the field.

Anxious to see what the new piece of artillery would do, Marion instructed Major Eaton to plant the little six-pounder on a rise of ground where it could rake the northern face of Fort Motte's stockade. Colonel Lee meanwhile placed the troops in position to charge when needed.

Mrs. Motte presently came to Marion with a trusted slave who had news for the General: That very morning, an hour or so before the Americans came, Captain MacPherson had received reinforcements of a small detachment of dragoons sent from Charleston. The slave said they might number as many as sixteen horses and men. Marion did not mind, but he was glad the troops were horsemen and not artillery.

By early afternoon Major Eaton and his men were ready to start bombarding the fort. The gun was in place. The gunners were standing by. Marion was not, however, quite ready to begin the battle.

First, as he had done at Fort Watson, this humane

The vivacious Mrs. Motte greeted the Americans joyfully.

officer would give the enemy a chance to surrender without bloodshed. He sent an officer with a flag to call upon Captain MacPherson and to say that immediate surrender would save many lives, both British and American.

Captain MacPherson sent his compliments to General Marion and declined the offer.

There was nothing more to be done. General Marion approached the waiting gunners. "Major Eaton," said he, "you may fire when you are ready."

In another instant the little six-pounder belched smoke. The ball screamed viciously. The aim had been perfect. The ball struck the high stockade halfway to its top. The logs shivered but did not give way. The ball bounced and rolled harmlessly down the hill.

Eaton's men reloaded, this time with a heavier charge of powder. Again the gun boomed, the projectile thudded against the stockade, then rolled away.

From the fort came yells of derision. The British, who may well have feared the gun, were elated. What good was a tiny brass cannon against the thick stout logs of their defenses?

For another half hour Major Eaton's gunners loaded and fired. The balls made not the least impression. It was clear Fort Motte was not to be taken in this manner.

As evening fell Marion and Lee called Major Maham. "Is there any chance here," Marion asked, "to build a tower, such as you did at Fort Watson?"

Maham had been looking over the ground with just such an idea. "No, sir, I fear not. I have observed the fort from every point. I cannot find a spot that would do."

The officers talked on into the night, discussing possible methods of attack other than an infantry charge, which Lee thought would be little more than suicide for the Americans.

While this council of war was taking place, a courier arrived from General Greene with serious news: Lord Rawdon, now commander in chief of the British army in the south, had left Camden with nearly two thousand soldiers. They were on the march south down the Wateree to support Captain MacPherson.

Here was a stunner! Marion's and Lee's force did not number more than two hundred men. The artillery bombardment had proved only that a six-pounder could not damage the stockade at the range attempted.

Colonel Lee suggested digging a trench to get as near the fort as possible, then charging the stockade and blowing an entry with gunpowder, or chopping one with axes.

Marion was not in favor of this plan. "Colonel,"

he protested, "before our men could get out of the trench to wreck the stockade, they would be murdered by musket fire."

"But what else can we do?" Lee demanded. "Rawdon's army is on the way. They will arrive at a point across the river from us in less than two days."

"So they will," replied Marion. "But they can't cross to our side here. They'll have to march on down to Nelson's Ferry before they can get across."

"Even so, General," warned Lee, "they can reach us in three days at most."

Marion had to agree that Lee was right. Marion knew there wasn't time to get a bigger gun from Greene. No one seemed to have any plan except Lee. Marion consented with reluctance to Lee's plan.

Colonel Lee went to call on Mrs. Motte. Could she provide him with digging tools? Indeed she could. "And," said she, "I can send you a party of strong Negroes who can dig a trench faster than your soldiers can."

Selecting the most powerful and energetic men, Mrs. Motte had them get shovels and go to work under Colonel Lee. They dug like fiends. After an hour or so, Lee sent them back to rest and set soldiers to digging. During the day the alternating parties brought the trench almost to within musket-shot of the fort.

In the afternoon one of Marion's scouts came in to report that Rawdon's advance guard had reached a point directly across the river from Fort Motte. They seemed to be going into camp. General Marion rode out early that evening and saw scores of camp-fires blinking in the dark. Rawdon was moving with almost incredible speed. Still, he and his men would have to march on to the ferry before they could cross over.

Marion and Lee felt uneasy. If after dark they could see the British army's fires, it was likely that Captain MacPherson from within Fort Motte could see them too, at least from the upper story of the Motte mansion. If so, then he would know that relief for his beleaguered garrison was not far off. Let him hold out another day and night, and Rawdon's fine cavalry surely would arrive to make short work of the Americans.

That is the way Lee and Marion figured it. These

two officers debated the problem far into the night: What could be done to force MacPherson to surrender, short of trying to blow up or chop through the stockade? Even if successful, this would be a bloody method, sure to cost many American lives.

"If we don't take the fort by tomorrow evening," Marion said, "we are not likely to take it at all. We'll have to get out of here before Rawdon's men begin arriving."

At this point Colonel Lee suggested a new idea. This, in the quaint language of an old account, was "To communicate fire to MacPherson's headquarters in the Motte mansion."

Before daylight the two officers went to see Mrs. Motte. Though roused from sleep, the widow was as alert as at midday when Lee explained matters to her. Rawdon's army was coming. The Americans must leave before Rawdon's mounted troopers came. Although another hour's digging would bring the trench pretty close to the stockade, an American attack on the stockade would be successful—if at all —only at a terrible cost of lives.

"Instead of risking so much," Colonel Lee con-

tinued, "we might be able to set fire to Captain Mac-
Pherson's headquarters."

"Why, then, Colonel," demanded Mrs. Motte, as
cool as could be, "do you not do so?"

"Madam, it is your mansion. It would be destroyed."

"By all means let it burn," replied the gallant
widow, "rather than have our soldiers killed!"

So spoke a true patriot. Colonel Lee bowed. General Marion nodded, and mumbled something. He
even smiled.

Dawn found Mrs. Motte's Negroes digging again
as if their lives depended on it. By noon the trench
was ready. General Marion sought out one of his
men, Private Nathan Savage, who was said to know
a great deal about bows and arrows. Before the war,
he had often hunted deer with them. "Young man,"
said Marion to the only archer in the brigade, "how
long will it take you to fashion a good bow and a
handful of arrows?"

The astonished private replied that although he
could make the arrows quickly enough, a good working bow was something else. It must be made from

seasoned wood. He doubted if he could find the kind of wood he needed.

"I can make a bow of green wood pretty quick," said he, "but it won't shoot so good." Marion thought even a green bow would do. "Go, then, and make the best bow you can," he said, "and half a dozen arrows.

Dawn found Mrs. Motte's Negroes digging again.

Then come to me." He explained to Private Savage what the plan was. "It's Injun-style," he said, "and you are going to get the chance to set the redcoats' headquarters on fire."

Young Savage was bug-eyed and wildly happy. He

tore off to seek wood and a few feathers, a piece of cobbler's wax and some linen thread.

Marion and Lee were in Mrs. Motte's farmhouse when, a little later, Private Savage came in to report and to display the weapons he had made so quickly. The feathered arrows, he explained, were light and true. "But this bow ain't going to carry very far," he said. "It's too limber. Not much kick in it."

Mrs. Motte overheard the conversation. She dashed into a shed near the house, returning a moment later carrying an enormous bow and a bundle of strange-looking arrows.

"General Marion," said the widow patriot, "I've had these things many years but could never," she laughed, "find any use for them." She put them into Private Savage's hands. "Are they any good?" she asked.

The young archer knew at once that these were not the work of American Indians. But they looked like splendid weapons. "Where did they come from?" he asked.

"Somewhere in the East Indies," Mrs. Motte replied. "Possibly from Malay."

"I knew they wasn't Cherokee."

"Will they do?"

"Yes, ma'am, they'll do fine," said Private Savage.

General Marion spoke. "Got your fire-stuff ready?" he asked.

"Yes, sir, ready."

It was early afternoon when young Savage, the East Indian bow and arrows in hand, walked with Colonel Lee to the spot where the trench began. "My lad," said the Colonel, "stop here a minute. Now

"These will do fine," the young archer said.

take a good look at the big house. Note where it stands in relation to the far end of this trench."

The young man with the bow did as he had been bade.

"You should still be able to see the top of the mansion," Lee went on. "That is your target. The roof. The shingles are as dry as old cedar. Get your arrows onto that roof and burning. That is your job."

"Yes, sir. Have no fear. This is a smart bow."

"Good enough, young man. Make that roof burn smart, too."

With Colonel Lee's parting command in his ears, Private Nathan Savage of Marion's men went down into the trench, while General Marion and the rest of the brigade stood at arms in the open field, ready for whatever might happen. They were as silent as so many statues.

· X ·

THE BRIGADE USES
BOW AND ARROWS

Without a pause, as though he knew right where he was going and what he was to do, Private Nathan Savage walked to the far end of the trench, then stopped.

Leaning the big powerful bow against a wall of the ditch and laying six arrows carefully on the ground, he got out his flint and steel and a handful of fine cedar shavings. They were as dry, he may have reflected, as his mouth had suddenly become.

Without haste he struck a spark and caught it on

the shavings. He selected a long arrow whose point
he had already prepared with a mixture of resin and
brimstone. He held it a moment in the flame. The
arrow point flared. Putting arrow to bow, he pulled
strong and steady till the feather-end of the arrow
was back of his right ear, then he let go.

It was a beauty of a shot. Truer than a musket ball,
the flaming arrow streaked straight up and struck
the roof of British headquarters more than halfway

He pulled strong and steady . . . then he let go.

to the ridgepole. It stuck there, burning fiercely.

From his place in the trench young Savage heard cries and shouts. They came from the rear, not the front. The brigade had seen the arrow and was giving him a cheer. Savage leaned down to ignite a second arrow, then he shot. It struck the roof just where he had meant it to—lower down than the first and a little to one side. The archer paused just long enough to note that it, too, was burning.

By now the man in the trench could hear yelling from inside the fort. The British had seen what was happening. The cheering from the rear increased. Again Savage pulled mightily on the bow. He was still fair on the target. The dry roof was afire in three places. Smoke was starting to roll up high above the mansion.

Marion's men, standing ready in the field, were having a wonderful show. They could see the redcoats running wildly about, forming a bucket brigade to pass water up hand over hand to douse the flames. Ladders slammed on the roof. The firemen climbed.

General Marion had been standing near Major Eaton and the six-pounder. As the redcoat firemen

The redcoats were trying to douse the flames.

took their places on the roof, Marion gave the order to fire.

The little gun roared. A ball struck fair in the middle of the burning roof, leaving a hole a man could crawl through. The Americans were roaring. What a show!

Eaton's gunners reloaded quickly. They let go another round. This time it was a charge of grapeshot that rattled like hail on the shingles. The redcoats fell over themselves trying to get off the roof.

Captain MacPherson, a gallant commander, nevertheless knew when he was beaten. Up on a pole at his headquarters went a white flag. Marion's men joined the redcoats in putting out the fire. The British surrendered Fort Motte.

It was perhaps as odd a battle as any during the entire war; to win it the Americans had used "modern" artillery and also the bow and arrow of ancient times. Major Eaton and his little brass gun, and Private Savage with his long bow, were its heroes.

Its heroine, surely, was the Widow Motte, who had urged the Americans to set her own property on fire.

That evening, after the British surrender, Mrs. Motte invited "both the victorious and the captive officers" to be her guests at what an old account said was "a sumptuous dinner at her table, over which she presided with all the coolness and easy politeness for which she was remarkable." There was much good talk, there were toasts, and jollity.

General Marion paroled MacPherson's troops, some of whom promptly left Fort Motte to join Lord Rawdon's army that was then going into camp at Nelson's Ferry. It was as near to Fort Motte as that British officer got.

Word of the fall of Fort Motte had reached Rawdon before MacPherson's garrison came in. Not only that, but scouts had informed Rawdon that General Greene himself, with "a large force," was approaching Nelson's Ferry. This report greatly exaggerated the actual fact: Greene was indeed in the neighborhood but with only a small troop of horsemen. What had brought him there so suddenly was his anxiety to know what was happening at Fort Motte, for he had known Rawdon was hastening to support MacPherson.

False though it was, the report of Greene "and a large force" caused Rawdon to quit Nelson's Ferry at once and to retreat south with his army nearer to British-held Charleston.

General Greene, happy to know at first-hand of the American victory at Fort Motte, paused with General Marion only long enough to order Colonel Lee and his Legion to march north and join Colonel Thomas Sumter. Sumter and Lee were then to attack a small British garrison holding Fort Granby, thirty-two miles upriver from Motte.

Greene told Marion that the British force at Georgetown had been reduced until now it mustered no more than one hundred men. Could Marion, now that Lee had left him, recruit enought strength to attack Georgetown?

As noncommittal as ever, the Swamp Fox took a sip of his vinegar water and said merely that he would do what he could. That was all Greene, who understood the strange little commander perfectly, needed to know. He rode away north and west to join his main army. Now that Rawdon had been forced to retreat south, Greene planned to attack Ninety-Six.

General Marion, for all his casualness, was eager for another try at Georgetown. It will be remembered that he and Lee had once attempted to take that post, and had failed. So, detaching Major Maham and a small troop of cavalry to keep an eye on Rawdon's movements, the Swamp Fox moved his small brigade east across the Santee, and marched toward Georgetown.

Because the brigade now numbered no more than eighty-odd men, Marion soon went into camp. He sent couriers out to locate his furloughed soldiers who had gone home to carry on their spring farm work just before the attack on Fort Watson.

The boys responded in numbers to cheer Marion's heart. Within a few days, when the march on Georgetown was resumed, the brigade mustered one hundred and seventy men.

Expecting at any time to meet British outposts, Marion rode ahead with his advance guard as they approached Georgetown. But no resistance whatever was met. And when the whole brigade reached the town's fortifications, Marion learned that the British garrison had fled the night before and had sailed for Charleston. The post was taken without a shot.

It must have given General Marion no little satisfaction to march into Georgetown and be hailed as its liberator. Most if not all of the town's Tories had fled the place along with the British soldiers. The local patriots cheered the brigade as their deliverers. Never again would Georgetown be a port where supplies were landed for the redcoats.

For the next several days Marion's men lived well on British provisions left behind. Each got a new blanket. All drank their first coffee in many months, some for the first time. New flints were available for their muskets.

To add to their high spirits, good news came. Sumter and Lee had taken Fort Granby after a brief hard fight. Another dispatch told that General Greene was laying siege to Ninety-Six.

Then bad news came: Three fresh regiments of British troops debarked at Charleston and marched to join Lord Rawdon, who had gone into camp at Moncks Corner. Then, at the head of more than two thousand soldiers, Rawdon left Moncks to relieve the British garrison at Ninety-Six. This was now commanded by Colonel John Harris Cruger, a New York Tory both brave and able.

General Greene's besieging force of five hundred men gave up the attempt to take Ninety-Six and retired to the high hills of the Santee. It seemed like a defeat for the Americans. But was it? As soon as

General Marion was hailed as a liberator in Georgetown.

Rawdon arrived, he proceeded immediately to demolish Ninety-Six's strong fortifications and to abandon the place.

Ninety-Six had, since Cornwallis established it, commanded all operations of the British in South Carolina. Now Rawdon thought it best to get out of there. It was the very last British post in the far inland region of South Carolina. General Greene's threat had been responsible for its destruction and abandonment.

Having done away with Ninety-Six, Rawdon moved his main army down to the forks of the Edisto River, where he went into camp near Orangeburg. He was physically ill. His health, never robust, had been shattered by exposure and the worries of command. Now he formally resigned from the army and took ship for England. His place was taken by Colonel Alexander Stuart, a professional soldier with the reputation of being "a sturdy fighter."

It was almost time for the summer rains, but before the lowlands were flooded there was still time for some brisk fighting. At Moncks Corner the small commands of Marion, Lee and Thomas Sumter combined to hit the British post there and capture more than a hundred prisoners. They also took two hundred horses and a wagon train of supplies. The remnant of the British garrison was glad to get away alive. They withdrew into Charleston.

Now the rains came, an almost continuous torrential downpour that so swelled the rivers they overflowed their banks. Until the waters should recede, there could be little more fighting in the South.

In the high hills of the Santee General Greene and his men relaxed gratefully. Sweltering July passed. August came with little relief. Colonel Stuart seemed in no more haste than the Americans to resume fighting.

During this lull in the far South, the war in the North was ruthlessly moving toward its great climax in Virginia. France had sent soldiers and a mighty fleet to aid the Americans.

Lord Cornwallis was concentrating his entire strength in one small section of Virginia.

The brilliant young Frenchman, General Lafayette, kept feinting against Cornwallis, falling back
when threatened, then feinting again. It could not go
on forever. As soon as he could spare them, General
George Washington dispatched General Anthony
Wayne and his Pennsylvania Line troops across the
Potomac. With Wayne's more than one thousand
foot soldiers went the 4th Continental Artillery of
nine guns.

The commands of Wayne and Lafayette moved
eastward in Virginia as if to challenge Cornwallis
who, at least for the moment, chose to withdraw to
a strong position to see what the enemy planned to
do.

By land and by sea other Continental forces were
moving toward Virginia. So was the French fleet,
which presently stood off the entrance to Chesapeake
Bay, as if to prevent British warships from entering
with reinforcements and supplies for Cornwallis.

As for Cornwallis, he had moved his army to the
Yorktown Peninsula, and there he proceeded to throw
up immense fortifications.

Most of the American strength now seemed centered on Virginia, and especially the Yorktown district. If Nathanael Greene was to stage a showdown fight with Colonel Stuart and the British army in the far South, he would have to do so pretty much with the men he had.

At about the same time Cornwallis began throwing up breastworks in Virginia, the British army in the South, in command of Stuart, moved out from its Orangeburg camp where it had been resting during the heavy rains.

Word of this stirring reached General Greene from a spy who had actually watched while the British went into a new camp near a place called Eutaw Springs—soon to become famous in American history. The spy estimated Stuart's force to exceed two thousand men.

Eutaw Springs was less than twenty miles from where Greene was encamped at Lauren's Plantation. Greene made no move either to retreat or to attack the larger force. What he did was to send riders with urgent dispatches for Marion and two other bush-whacker commanders, Pickens and Harden, and to Light-Horse Harry Lee. The dispatches were alike: Come with your men as soon as you can to Burdell's Tavern. This was Greene's headquarters not far from Eutaw Springs.

· XI ·

THE BATTLE OF
EUTAW SPRINGS

The orders General Greene dispatched from his head-quarters near Eutaw Springs set in motion virtually all of the American forces left in the Deep South.

And because the Battle of Eutaw Springs was to be the last major battle of the war in South Carolina, let us see what the place was like in September, 1781. There were two of the springs, several rods apart. The water of both bubbled up cold, limpid and sparkling, almost fountain-like, from an underground stream. From the second or lower spring, the water formed

Eutaw Creek which flowed about two miles before entering the Santee River.

The springs were on a large plantation, and near them at that time stood the fine brick mansion of the planter. In this house the British commander, Colonel Alexander Stuart, had set up his headquarters. Inclosing the mansion, together with its garden and orchard and many acres of field, was a palisade. Within this protection, camped in tents, were more than two thousand redcoats.

Shaded by tall cypresses and oaks, Eutaw Springs plantation was much like a beautiful park, a perfect spot for tired soldiers to relax in comparative safety from the enemy. Where *was* the enemy, anyway?

Colonel Stuart and his men may well have been so soothed by the peaceful, almost dreamy atmosphere of the place, that even their scouts and pickets were lulled. In any case, not one of them had the least knowledge of what was taking place on Burdell's plantation, less than seven miles from Eutaw Springs.

To the tavern on the Burdell place, for three days running, couriers had been coming with dispatches for General Greene reporting the approach of this or that body of American troops. General Marion's brigade was the first to come, on September 5th. Others were close behind. Among them were two battalions of North Carolina militia under Colonel Francis Malmedy, and one battalion of South Carolina militia under Colonel Pickens.

Colonel Lee's Legion was coming. So were Ortho Williams and John Howard, veterans of the Cowpens, with their Continentals. Colonel William Washington rode at the head of his regiment of seasoned horse soldiers.

Other American brigades or regiments, led by William Henderson, Jethro Sumner and Wade Hampton, were reported nearby. So was Robert Kirkwood with a body of Delaware troops.

Although the company rosters of the bushwhackers and the militia were notoriously inaccurate, General Greene looked at his reports and was pleased. Even allowing for possible error, it looked as if he could put two thousand men into the coming battle.

Stuart's army totaled perhaps a few hundred less than two thousand. It surely contained many more trained soldiers than the Americans could boast. Still,

Greene felt he had a good chance against the professional soldiers, especially if he were able to stage a surprise attack.

On the evening of September 7th, General Greene prepared to strike at Stuart early the next morning. The front line of advance was to be four battalions of militia, in two columns—one commanded by General Marion, the other by Colonel Malmedy. Marion's own brigade was to head the first column. It was to be the brigade's first formal battle. Their commander was not at all sure how his Injun-style warriors would perform.

Dawn of the 8th was to be a terrible shock to the complacent British. Nothing to ruffle their peace had occurred during the night. Stuart felt so secure that at daylight he sent one hundred men, *without arms,* and accompanied only by a small troop of cavalry, out of camp along the road to Burdell's. They were to forage for potatoes and greens.

While these men were digging away like so many farmers, two American deserters came through the lines. They were taken direct to Eutaw Springs where they reported to General Stuart that even then General Greene was marching to attack the British camp. Thinking the deserters were spies, Stuart had them locked up in his guardhouse.

But something or other then caused Stuart to have a second thought; perhaps there was some truth in what the two men had said. Stuart snapped out an order, and the men of Colonel John Coffin's regiment, just then eating breakfast, were told to form up. It took a few minutes, but they got their muskets and were soon in marching order, both horse and foot soldiers, moving out on the road toward Burdell's.

In another half an hour Colonel Coffin, at the head of his column, saw scores of men running toward him, all unarmed. Right at their heels were horse soldiers, shooting at the erstwhile potato diggers. The horsemen were South Carolinians from General Marion's column.

Colonel Coffin, thinking he had come upon only the advance guard of Greene's army, put his men into a charge. Marion immediately ordered his horsemen to fall back. They did. Coffin, now sure he was facing only a small detachment, sent his troops to chasing the Americans. He couldn't see that farther down the road was Colonel Lee's Legion of steel-tempered infantry and cavalry, together with the rest of Marion's column, moving ahead through the cover of woods beside the road.

It was then that Marion and Lee hit Coffin with everything they had. The woods on each side of the British exploded with musket fire, and coming through the smoke were foot soldiers on the double in a bayonet charge. It was too much for Coffin's surprised and outnumbered men. They stopped, they started to fall back, and at last they turned and got out of there as fast as they could.

Back at the British camp, Colonel Stuart heard the distant shooting. His second guess had been right; there was trouble on the road to Burdell's. He went into instant action to make up for the mistake of permitting a surprise attack. Drums beat. Bugles sounded orders.

Field guns were wheeled into position to command the road. The British 3rd Regiment of East Kents, together with the 63rd Manchesters, all splendid

Marion's foot soldiers came through in a bayonet charge.

troops, formed long lines well outside the camp, their flank resting on the bank of Eutaw Creek.

But Greene's men did not stop. Marion's and Pickens's brigades, in the center, were coming ahead fast in the face of steady fire. Lee and Henderson covered the flanks. Back of this front line were the soldiers of Hampton, Williams and Sumner.

The American artillery of four small guns was rolled up to fire on the British fieldpieces which were raking the advance, killing or wounding many of Malmedy's North Carolina militia. Though two British guns were hit and disabled, Malmedy's men had been hard hit. They began to yield. General Greene saw the danger, and sent in Jethro Sumner's regiment to hold the line. Colonel Stuart sent in a reserve regiment to press the British advantage. The Americans began to fall back.

Greene was in a desperate position and he knew it. He called for Ortho Williams and his Continentals. "Like a full-winged storm," says an old account, "these experienced troops swept forward until they were within forty yards of the redcoats." Then they paused to let go a destructive volley.

It staggered the British. Then, in came the second line of Williams's men with naked bayonets. The redcoats faltered. They were badly hurt. Captain Ruduloph of Lee's Legion saw the big opportunity. Instantly he brought a company of Legionnaires into position to sweep the confused British with a flanking fire.

On another part of the smoking, roaring field, Colonel Howard led a charge against the famous 3rd

Regiment of East Kents. After one quick volley the two lines came together with bayonets.

Posted in a tangle of blackjack bushes, in reserve, was a company of seasoned British grenadiers in command of a tough and remarkable officer known to American history only as Major Majoribanks. Before Howard's Americans knew what struck them, Majoribanks's men came out from their cover and mowed down the Continentals with musket, sword and bayonet.

Coming up just then were Colonel William Washington and his cavalry. Noting a small open space between Majoribanks and the blackjack jungle, bold Washington decided to take his horsemen through it and hit Majoribanks from the rear. But that alert Briton turned his grenadiers on their heels and met Washington's horsemen with gunfire. Washington's horse was shot dead under him. And as he fell, that brave officer was bayoneted by two grenadiers and captured.

Yet, except for Majoribanks, the whole British line was retreating, falling back on the camp near the brick house. Some of the men did not stop there but ran on for the woods beyond the inclosure. The battle seemed all but won for the Americans. One more charge and it would be all over.

General Greene ordered the charge, which was led by regiments of both Continental and militia troops. It went forward without a hitch. It swept on into the inclosure. In another moment the Americans found themselves among the British tents. That is not all they found. They found heaps of cooked food, ready to eat. And kegs of rum, ready to drink.

The American artillery of four small guns was

The famished soldiers paused to stuff themselves with food. Probably they thought the battle was already won. They knocked in the heads of the casks. Strong rum went down the gullets of the exhausted and jubilant Americans. In a flash, discipline went to pieces. As far as these fellows were concerned, all that remained to be done was to celebrate.

Before word got to Greene of the danger, Stuart learned of the orgy around the rum kegs. He was no man to miss an opportunity like this. He soon had a

rolled up to fire on the British fieldpieces.

small swivel gun in the second story of the brick house pouring a murderous fire down upon the Americans in the inclosure.

Greene called Marion to protect the two American field guns while their gunners could turn the weapons on the brick house. In this exposed position, Marion's men were under extremely heavy fire. He and they not only stood their ground but also captured a British six-pounder from the enemy artillerymen. Before it could be put into action, however, Stuart had rallied his retreating forces and was advancing.

What was more, Major Majoribanks with a fairly large number of his grenadiers suddenly appeared, as if from nowhere, in the garden near the brick house.

General Greene knew that one more good charge might have left the field to the Americans. He knew, too, that one more charge might have made a bare skeleton of his army. He could not afford so costly a victory. After all, his army was all right here at Eutaw Springs. He gave the order to retreat.

Save for the intoxicated, who were left where they still staggered or had fallen, the Americans performed an orderly withdrawal. Nor did Stuart attempt to harass them. He was content to remain on the field and repossess the camp he had so nearly lost.

With what must have been a heavy heart, Nathanael Greene led his bloody, battered troops back along the route they had marched four hours previously.

It had been one of the most hotly contested battles of the Revolution. The Americans could count one hundred thirty-nine killed, three hundred seventy-five wounded, and eight missing, making a total of five hundred twenty-two. The British lost eighty-five killed, three hundred fifty-one wounded, four hundred thirty missing.

Who had won the Battle of Eutaw Springs? You may take your choice. The British suffered far the greater losses but they remained on the field. The Americans retreated to their position on Burdell's plantation.

But the Battle of Eutaw Springs had a significance beyond the outcome of the battle itself. Although General Greene could not know it on that dismal, heartbreaking retreat to Burdell's, he had practically wrecked the British army in the South. Eutaw Springs was the climax of his campaign in which he

In this exposed position they were under heavy fire.

had forced the British to give up, one after the other, the chain of forts and posts all the way from the coast to the far inland garrison of Ninety-Six. And he had accomplished all this with the fragments of the defeated and discouraged army he had inherited from General Gates.

Recognition of this superb work was to come later. But now all Greene and his army could do was to bury their dead, lick their wounds, and wonder what Stuart meant to do.

As soon as Greene's forces had left the field, General Stuart went about burying his dead, among them the incomparable Major Majoribanks, and went into camp for the night.

· XII ·

END OF THE REVOLUTION

The morning after the battle saw the British making haste to retreat toward Charleston. Setting fire to his large store of supplies, Colonel Stuart put his shrunken, battered army on the road south. He even left seventy-two of his wounded to be cared for by the Americans.

General Greene and General Marion were already scouting the enemy's camp, and once they were certain the redcoats were leaving, Greene ordered Marion and Lee to follow and harass the retreat.

Taking such of the brigade as were fitted for it,

the Americans set out on the trail. But Stuart had sent an appeal for help to the British garrison in Charleston, and Major MacArthur with a thousand men moved forward so swiftly they met Stuart near Moncks Corner. All Marion and Lee could do in the face of such an army was to withdraw to a strong position and watch. Within a few days Greene ordered Marion to join him in the high hills of the Santee where he was moving his shattered troops to rest.

At a council of war, General Greene outlined the campaign to be followed. The main purpose of it was to keep the enemy confined to the Charleston district. The British had lost every inland post, one after the other—Ninety-Six, Camden, Fort Motte, Fort Watson—all of their garrison chain had fallen or been evacuated. It had been a slow and bitter process, and it had left the British holed up in the small district between the Cooper and Ashley rivers.

True, ammunition, arms, uniforms, and even medical supplies were reaching the besieged by ship. Yet they had a serious problem, which was fodder for their horses and food not only for the regular troops but also for the many hundreds of Tories who had swarmed into Charleston.

"If we can't get the men and the guns to drive them out," said General Greene, "we can starve them out."

Marion and Lee followed and harassed the retreat.

No commander in the North or South was more fit to make trouble for enemy foraging parties than the Swamp Fox. He knew every road, every plantation, every ford and ferry, every short cut.

Now that Stuart could see the possibility of being

bottled up for the winter, he set about in a last-minute effort to accumulate provisions and fodder. He was wary of Marion, well knowing that bushwhacker's ability to hit and run. For the moment, however, the Swamp Fox seemed to have disappeared.

Marion was busy enough, though so quietly did he move that the British could find no trace of him. Then, without warning, his men rode out of the swamp mists and hit one of Stuart's parties at Fairlawn. They ran off the British horses, shot up the strong guard, and destroyed a wagon train of food and fodder. After that, Marion again disappeared.

Then, on November 9, while Marion and his men were resting in camp near Huger's Bridge, official word came of the surrender of Lord Cornwallis and his entire army at Yorktown. This had happened weeks before, or on the 19th of October, 1781.

By the same courier came a dispatch for General Marion. In it the Congress of the United States cited him for "his wise and gallant conduct in defending the liberties of his country," and went on to stress "the distinguished part" General Marion had taken at the Battle of Eutaw Springs.

Though never much given to ceremony, Marion felt that the great event at Yorktown called for some sort of recognition, even here in the remote back country. After all, it meant that the war really was over. So, next evening at the house of John Cantey, General Marion gave what was described as "a fine party for the ladies of Santee."

General Greene had of course been the first to receive the news of Yorktown. The surrender of Cornwallis meant that the British in South Carolina were virtually the only active enemy troops left in the country.

Well, then, short of powder and lead as he was, to say nothing of insufficient soldiers, Greene would act to prevent Stuart from accomplishing anything. In a quick march he suddenly appeared close to the British outpost of Charleston at Dorchester. The officer in command was jittery. Without waiting for Greene to attack, he burned his supplies, wheeled his two pieces of artillery into the Ashley River, and led his men on the double to the protection of the city.

Greene was amazed. With less than four rounds of ammunition per man, here he was going into camp, within twenty miles of Charleston, without having fired a shot. He hoped that Stuart did not suspect the real condition of his tiny army. Stuart didn't. He made no attempt to dislodge Greene at Dorchester.

Greene posted strong pickets around his camp, and waited for the Continental reinforcements which he expected would soon come from Virginia, now that the war had ended in the North.

The British now changed commanders. Colonel Stuart was relieved. In his place was General Alexander Leslie who arrived by ship with fresh troops. One of Greene's spies, who saw Leslie disembark at Charleston, returned to report that the British now had more than three thousand redcoat regulars in that city, and also several hundred Tories in uniform.

Greene resolved to make a bold attack in the hope of causing the new British commander to think the Americans were far stronger than they were. The target was an enemy garrison on John's Island close to

Charleston, in command of Major Craig, who had five hundred men and four guns. It was to be a night attack, a surprise.

The attack miscarried. The Americans were obliged to retire. Yet the threat had served its purpose. Major Craig immediately abandoned the position and fled with his men into Charleston.

Little by little, Greene's inadequate forces were hemming the redcoats into their last stand in all South Carolina.

There had been no civil government in South Carolina for more than two years, or almost since John Rutledge was elected governor. Now, with the enemy confined to one spot, Rutledge and General Greene sought to reëstablish the legislative assembly. To do so would show the many Tories that the British were beaten, that it was time the Tories made up their minds either to turn patriot or to leave the state.

With this in mind, Rutledge and Greene agreed it would be most effective for the assembly to meet virtually under the noses of the enemy. Greene promptly moved his army across the Edisto River to the small community named Jacksonborough, which was no more than thirty miles from the British lines.

The governor issued a proclamation: Let the citizens of South Carolina call meetings wherever they could and elect delegates to the assembly. The election was something of a hit-or-miss affair, and more soldiers than civilians managed to vote, yet it was the best that could be done in the circumstances.

To hold the assembly at Jacksonborough was a bold move. It worked, too. General Leslie did not lift a hand to attack the community. The newly elected senators and representatives made their way to the little town, which became the temporary capital of the state. Among them was Senator Francis Marion of St. John's Parish, Berkeley County.

Before leaving for the assembly, Marion split his brigade into two commands, one under Colonel Hezekiah Maham, the other under Colonel Peter Horry. They had orders to continue to prevent provisions from entering Charleston.

At least twice during the legislative session, Marion

was called into the field to head the brigade during emergencies. One of these occurred when Major Gainey, the Tory leader, made a last supreme effort to stage an uprising of Tories in the Pee Dee district.

Getting into his fighting clothes, Marion led his horsemen on a swift dash and caught Gainey's growing mob off guard. Without the firing of more than a few shots, they compelled the surrender of five hundred armed Tories. Then, near where the town of Marion stands today, Marion offered them their freedom on condition that they take the oath to support the government of South Carolina. It was the last Tory rising of any consequence.

From this point on, it was Marion's practice to conciliate Tories. Their cause was lost. Instead of holding a grudge, why not give them a chance to become good Americans? Nor was he inclined to attack the redcoats unless forced by circumstances to do so.

Marion's attitude was made clear by an incident: When the British were starting preparations to give up Charleston, General Greene wrote Marion suggesting that he attack a group of men engaged in cutting wood for the enemy. Marion did not attack. The war was over, he reasoned. Let the British go as soon as they could.

Instead of harassing the woodcutters, therefore, he sent a detail of his trusted men to protect them from being shot by members of the brigade who were still so bitter they could not resist an opportunity to cut down the enemy.

"Enough blood has already been shed," Marion told a friend. "I shall not spill another drop of it— unless Americans are attacked."

The year 1782 wore steadily away. General Marion and his men made their camp for many weeks on the deserted plantation of a Tory, Sir John Colleton, on Wadboo Creek. It was there, too, when the British were at last about to take ship to leave Charleston, that Marion thanked his officers and men "and bid them an affectionate farewell." The brigade was a thing of the past.

On December 14, the British got aboard the vessels

They took the oath to support the government of South Carolina.

sent to take them home. As the last ship weighed anchor, General Greene's army came marching into the city.

Marion's brigade was not among the troops that witnessed the ceremony of the victorious entry of the Americans. Neither was any other unit of the bushwhacking militia. The reason for this shameful exclusion, by order of the South Carolina civil authority, is not clear. It was said officially to be because of fear that "the hard-to-manage partisan troops might cause trouble by attacking the embarking Redcoats."

At eleven o'clock, on that great day of December, 1782, a detachment of American soldiers took formal possession of the town. At three in the afternoon General Nathanael Greene escorted the new governor of the state, John Matthews, and other civil officers, to the town hall.

"From windows," says an old account, "from balconies, from housetops, the troops were greeted with cheers, the waving of handkerchiefs, and cries of 'God bless you, gentlemen!' "

Before nightfall, the British squadron of some three hundred vessels crossed the bar, and "the last speck of canvas of that hostile array glittered far out on the ocean . . ."

By the time Charleston was free of the late enemy, Francis Marion was riding for Pond Bluff, the modest plantation he had left to organize and lead his brigade. Though he couldn't know it then, that brigade had taken its shining place in South Carolina legend and in the larger history of the American war for liberty.

· XIII ·

OLD SOLDIER AT HOME

Pond Bluff, like many another plantation whose owner had gone away to the war, was in desperate condition. Situated in St. John's Parish which for nearly three years had been the scene of marches, encampments and battles, it had been raided again and again by redcoats and Tories.

Of Marion's twenty Negroes, only ten remained. Virtually all the farm implements had disappeared. There was no grain left, there were no cattle, pigs or poultry. Several of the buildings had been wantonly burned. Others were in disrepair. Marion himself was somewhat in disrepair from the brutal life common to bushwhacking soldiers. He was fifty years old.

Yet the same determination that had kept him fighting without pay, often without food or even ammunition, for what must have seemed a hopeless cause, did not now desert him. Little by little, with the help of his faithful Negroes, Pond Bluff was restored to something approaching its pre-war condition.

Meanwhile, Marion was twice reëlected to the South Carolina senate. In 1784 the legislature, in gratitude for his incomparable services, provided him with the command of Fort Johnson, one of the restored harbor defenses of Charleston. A small salary, a sort of pension, accompanied the position.

In the same year, however, Marion resigned the Fort Johnson post to marry a cousin, Miss Mary Esther Videau, a charming and well-to-do spinster. At Pond Bluff the couple built a comfortable home "with one sitting room but many chambers." The house was of durable cypress. It was never painted.

This seems typical of a man who although a general never troubled himself about a uniform of rank, and never wore a hat other than the battered and scorched helmet with which he began military service—the same little headpiece with the silver crescent of the South Carolina 2nd Regiment.

Here in his modest home the old soldier enjoyed entertaining the comrades of wartime, and others. All found "a hearty welcome and good cheer," and "the stranger never failed to find hospitality."

At the state constitutional convention of 1790, General Marion took his seat as one of the most distinguished and popular members. A year later he was again reëlected to the state senate.

Friends and visitors to the general's home noticed that among his most valued possessions were the old camp bed and cooking utensils he had carried, like any common private, during the war. His faithful servant Oscar, who had accompanied him throughout all the raids and forays, survived to enjoy the reflected glory of a master who was steadily growing into a national legend.

Francis Marion died at Pond Bluff on February 27, 1795, and was buried with honors at Belle Isle, where he had formerly lived with a brother. For many years the acres of Pond Bluff have been hidden beneath the waters of Lake Marion, a hydroelectric project which supplies power to a large part of the state. There is also a national forest named for Marion in his native commonwealth.

There are no less than thirty towns and cities in the United States named Marion, and five more places named Marion Center, Marion Junction, or Marion Heights. It seems probable that most if not all of these were named expressly to honor the memory of the South Carolina hero. Even in distant Oregon, as long ago as 1849, the Territorial legislature voted unanimously to change the name of Champoeg County to Marion County. This was done, says a contemporary report, because the character of General Marion greatly appealed to the Oregon pioneer settlers.

In his native South Carolina, whose people have long memories and are given to cherishing remembrances of the heroes of the past, Francis Marion stands superb and unique—The Swamp Fox of the Revolution.

Perhaps no epitaph fits him better than the characterization voiced by one of his own soldiers. "General Marion," said this member of the famous brigade, "was part rawhide and part vinegar, wrapped around the biggest heart on the Continent."

BIBLIOGRAPHY

Bass, Robert D., *The Green Dragoon*, New York, 1957.

Dictionary of American Biography, 22 Vols., New York, 1928-1944.

James, William Dobein, *A Sketch of the Life of Brig. Gen. Francis Marion and a History of His Brigade from Its Rise in June, 1780, Until Disbanded in December, 1782*, Charleston, S. C., 1821; reprinted at Marietta, Ga., 1948.

Lancaster, Bruce, *From Lexington to Liberty*, New York, 1955.

Lossing, Benson J., *The Pictorial Field-Book of the Revolution*, Vol. 2, New York, 1855.

Simms, W. Gilmore, *Life of Francis Marion*, Philadelphia, 1809.

Williams, Beryl, and Epstein, Samuel, *Francis Marion*, New York, 1956.

INDEX